D0439603

San Antonio Uncovered

Mark Louis Rybczyk

Wordware Publishing, Inc.

REGIONAL DIVISION

Library of Congress Cataloging-in-Publication Data

Rybczyk, Mark Louis.
    San Antonio uncovered / by Mark Louis Rybczyk.
        p.   cm.
    ISBN 1-55622-145-2
    1. San Antonio (Tex.)—History.   2. San Antonio (Tex.)—Description.
I. Title.
F394.S2R93   1991
976.4'351—dc20   91-20146
                                                                   CIP

Copyright © 1992, Wordware Publishing, Inc.

All Rights Reserved

1506 Capital Avenue
Plano, Texas 75074

No part of this book may be reproduced in any form or by any means
without permission in writing from Wordware Publishing, Inc.

Printed in the United States of America

ISBN 1-55622-145-2
10 9 8 7 6 5 4 3 2
9107

All inquiries for volume purchases of this book should be addressed to
Wordware Publishing, Inc., at the above address. Telephone inquiries
may be made by calling:
                    (214) 423-0090

CONTENTS

Photo credits:

The Institute of Texan Cultures, San Antonio Texas
The *San Antonio Light* Collection

Fort Sam Houston Military Museum

University of Texas at Dallas

"San Antonio is, next to San Francisco and New Orleans and possibly Boston, the most colorful and romantic city in America."

John Geunther
Inside USA

Introduction

It has often been said that much of history falls through the cracks. If that is true, then this book is historical caulking. When you thumb through this book, you will notice that the missions and the Alamo are rarely mentioned. Many fine books have been written about those subjects, and I have chosen not to duplicate those efforts. I prefer to concentrate on off-the-wall subjects, such as the story of the Travis Club Cigar or the tale of the ladies bathroom at the Alamo Heights Mobil gas station. Separately, these stories mean very little; yet, when woven together, they help explain the complex fabric of life in San Antonio.

Ask any person who has lived in San Antonio for some time about the city, and you will discover that he possesses a wealth of stories about San Antonio. This book is a collection of those tales.

Who is this book for? First of all, it is for the lifelong resident of San Antonio who has always wondered, whatever happened to the roller coaster at Playland Park? It is for the middle-aged, who long for the days of the giant Santa Claus atop the downtown Joske's. It is for every man and woman who feels that the downtown skyline is not the same without the old Alamo National Bank sign.

Secondly, this book was written for the newly arrived San Antonian, the nonnative, Texan by choice. Too many times in these days of freeways and subdivisions, a newcomer will move to San Antonio and plop his family down in loopland

and wonder, what is so special about this place? There is nothing special about a part of town that features fast food restaurants, strip shopping centers, and access roads. His new surroundings are similar to any other Sunbelt boom-town. I am constantly amazed by the number of people who have lived in San Antonio for five or ten years who have visited the Alamo, have taken the out-of-town relatives to the River Walk, but have never visited the Quadrangle. They have never stopped at Sunken Gardens or have never seen (or for that matter heard of) the old Spanish Aqueduct. This book is a crash course in local culture.

And, finally, this book is for the frequent visitor to the Alamo City. Thousands flock each year to our humble town, spend a few days visiting the River Walk, Sea World, and the Alamo, and then return home. So often, they miss the point of San Antonio.

I once heard a Dallas resident say that San Antonio is a small town desperately wanting to be a big city. He could not have been farther from the truth. San Antonio is a big city (over one million people) that desperately wants to be a small town. It is a town that cries when a small tacky hole in the wall known as Hipp's Bubble Room passes into oblivion. It is a collection of people who celebrate the saving of the Majestic and the old Fairmount Hotel and gather in the streets to watch it being moved. It is a bicultural city that revels in the differences of its people rather than quarrels over them. This, I believe, is the essence of San Antonio.

Mark Louis Rybczyk

How much do you really know about San Antonio? Test your knowledge . . . . . .

1. What was the name of the Irish Neighborhood that prospered in San Antonio in the late 1800s?
2. What former U.S. president was at one time a football and baseball coach at St. Mary's University?
3. In what San Antonio hotel did Teddy Roosevelt recruit his Rough Riders?
4. What was the name of the first film to win an Academy Award for best picture? Where was its premiere?
5. Where did John Wayne's film *The Alamo* premiere?
6. La Mansion Del Rio Hotel was originally the home of what local institution?
7. What three-story hotel was once moved three blocks downtown, setting a world record for the largest building ever moved?
8. Who built the parapet and the roof to the Alamo chapel?
9. What is the name of the ancient ditches that supplied water to the missions?
10. What popular snack food originated in San Antonio?
11. What is the second oldest park in the United States?
12. What is the third oldest park in the United States?
13. What military installation was once known as the West Point of the Air?
14. What famous Indian was once held captive at Ft. Sam Houston's Quadrangle?
15. Name the device that was successfully demonstrated at Military Plaza that changed the cattle industry forever?
16. What downtown city park is actually a cemetery?
17. What San Antonio high school was once described in *Life Magazine* as "most outstanding modern school in the U.S."?
18. The San Antonio Museum of Art is housed in a building that was once the home of what local institution?
19. What San Antonio landmark was once off-limits to military personnel?

20. What downtown building was once the tallest building west of the Mississippi River?

Part B: For Masters Only

1. Name the only San Antonio team to play in the Cotton Bowl.
2. Who laid the cornerstone at St. Mark's Episcopal Church downtown?
3. What was the name of San Antonio's entry in the National Bowling League?
4. Who visited San Antonio on September 13, 1987?
5. What is engineeringly significant about the Espada Dam?
6. The San Antonio Blue Book was a commercial directory for what type of business?
7. What public housing project was the first in the United States?
8. What was the nickname of the last baseball team to occupy Mission Stadium?
9. What is unusual about the clock tower at the old Ursuline Academy?
10. The facade of the San Pedro Playhouse is a replica of what vanished local landmark?
11. Who graduated at the top of his class among aviation cadets at Kelly Field in 1925?
12. What local school did Douglas MacArthur attend?
13. Daniel Boone once owned what piece of downtown property?
14. John Ebersol's company built three movie theatres in San Antonio, the Majestic being his finest. Name the other two.
15. What famous photographer was the first person to supply photos to both the *Light* and the *Express* newspapers?

16. Sculptor Gutzon Borglum had a studio on the San Antonio River where he created some of his finest pieces. What was his most famous work?
17. What was the fate of the "big sign" that towered over the Joske's downtown store in the 1930s?
18. Mike Souchak set what record at Brackenridge Park on February 20, 1955?
19. Benjamin Foulois is famous for what event?
20. What downtown hotel was constructed in such a revolutionary way that it was able to welcome guests before it was completed?

Match the person with their respective nickname

1.	General Jack Pershing	A.	The Flying Schoolgirl
2.	O. P. Schnabel	B.	The Iceman
3.	Josephine Lucchese	C.	Black Jack
4.	Henry B. Gonzales	D.	The Kansas Cyclone
5.	Dwight D. Eisenhower	E.	Old Pushbroom
6.	Katherine Stinson	F.	The Breadline Banker
7.	Emily Morgan	G.	Henry B.
8.	John Twohig	H.	The American Nightingale
9.	George Gervin	I.	The Yellow Rose

Answers

Part A

1. Irish Flats
2. Dwight D. Eisenhower
3. The Menger
4. *Wings*, The Texas Theatre
5. The Woodlawn Theatre
6. St. Mary's College
7. The Fairmount
8. The U.S. Army
9. Acequias
10. Fritos
11. San Pedro Park
12. Travis Park
13. Randolph Field
14. Geronimo
15. Barbed wire
16. Milam Park
17. Jefferson High School
18. The Lone Star Brewery
19. The River Walk
20. The Tower Life Building

0 - 5	correct	Sorry, you get a cascarone on the head.
5 - 10	correct	You obviously live in loopland.
10 - 15	correct	You deserve a raspa.
15 - 18	correct	You deserve a cerveza fria.
19 - 20	correct	You deserve a cerveza fria on me—don't stop now, if you get the next twenty right, I'll treat you to fajita dinner at the next NIOSA.

Part B

1. The Randolph Field Ramblers
2. Robert E. Lee
3. The Cavaliers
4. Pope John Paul II
5. It is curved the wrong way.
6. Brothels
7. Apache-Alazon Courts
8. The San Antonio Bullets
9. It only has a clock on three sides.
10. The old Market House
11. Charles Lindbergh
12. West Texas Military Academy
13. Bowen's Island
14. The Laurel and the Woodlawn
15. E. O. Goldbeck
16. Mount Rushmore
17. It was donated to a wartime scrap drive in 1942.
18. He set the PGA record for the lowest score for 72 holes at the 1955 Texas Open.
19. The first military flight ever, which occurred in 1911, at the Fort Sam Houston parade ground.
20. The Hilton

Part C Key

(1-C, 2-E, 3-H, 4-G, 5-D, 6-A, 7-I, 8-F, 9-B)

SECTION I

UNIQUELY SAN ANTONIO

Forgotten Facts About the Alamo

Perhaps no building is more symbolic of San Antonio than the Alamo. It is probably the most historic building in the state. Almost every Texan can recite the legend of the Alamo defenders, but few know the history of the Alamo after 1836. For instance, did you know that:

1. The Alamo is not a national historic site.
2. The famous parapet (the notable arched skyline), perhaps the architectural symbol of San Antonio, was added, 14 years after the battle, by the U.S. Army.

After the battle of the Alamo, the site was left as a ruin. Many people came to visit the shrine. Some took the stones as souvenirs; others sold trinkets that were made from pieces of the walls. In 1846 the U.S. Army began using the grounds as a quartermaster depot, but they left the chapel unused. When the Army made its first attempt to clear rubble from the site, skeletons were found.

In 1849 a three-way battle for control of the Alamo between the city, the Army, and the Catholic church hit the courts. It was not until 1855 that the Texas Supreme Court gave control of the Alamo to the Catholic church because the church had claim to the site from a "presumed grant from the Spanish Crown." Also seeking a claim to the Alamo lands was Samuel Maverick. Maverick was able to escape from the Alamo a few days before the battle and was sent as a delegate to the convention that declared Texas' independence. Maverick built a home on the northwest corner of the grounds. That site is now occupied by the Gibbs Building on the corner of Houston and Alamo. Maverick was also the first to prove that the Alamo was a mission and not a military fort. This decision helped the church eventually gain control.

Despite the fact that the Catholic church had regained control of the Alamo, the Army still occupied the site. Between 1850 and 1852 they made improvements to the chapel and added the famous parapet. The skyline was designed by architect John Fries and built by David Russi, a team that also built the First Presbyterian Church and the Market House. Some historians credit the Army and the contractors as the early force behind the restoration of the chapel. San Antonio at that time was populated mainly by German immigrants, Tejanos, and Catholics—three groups who had a view of the battle from a different perspective than the Anglo-American viewpoint that exists today.

It is probable that the Catholic church would have never converted the chapel into a shrine for Texas heroes. In fact, the Catholic church wanted to convert the Alamo into a place of worship for German Catholics. However, when St. Joseph's was built (a.k.a. St. Joske's), the Church's interest in the Alamo was only as a source of income from the Army's rent.

In 1877 Hugo Grenet purchased the convent area (known also as the barracks) for $20,000 and built a two-story store on the land. Grenet leased the chapel from the church and used it for storage. In 1882 Grenet died and the store was purchased by Hugo & Schmeltzer. The chapel was sold to the state of Texas in 1883 for $20,000.

One of the forgotten heroes of the Alamo was Adina DeZavala, granddaughter of Lorenzo DeZavala (first vice president of the Republic of Texas). DeZavala led the early fight to regain control of the convent area but could not raise enough money to purchase it. Clara Driscoll, recognized as the savior of the Alamo, entered the picture and purchased the area. The control of the convent area was given to the Daughters of the Republic of Texas. Unfortunately, the DRT was divided into two factions: one headed up by Clara Driscoll, one by DeZavala. The DeZavala group wanted to restore the convent area; the Driscoll group did not consider that an original part of the mission. The Driscoll faction eventually gained control, and their patriarch was the one whose place in history was eventually secured. Though DeZavala was forgotten in spite of her efforts, her mission to restore the convent area was eventually fulfilled.

A final note on Clara Driscoll—when she passed away in 1945, her body was laid in state in the Alamo chapel and later laid to rest in a city cemetery on the east side. Her tomb is just off Commerce Street in the southwest corner of one of the most neglected cemeteries in the city.

Aerial view of Alamo Plaza as it was in 1931. Notice the commercial structures that sit on the Alamo grounds.

The Truth About Davy Crockett's Tomb

In the rear of San Fernando Cathedral is a tomb that supposedly contains the remains of Davy Crockett, James Bowie, William Travis, and other heroes of the Alamo. A controversy that started over 100 years ago about the contents of the tomb has mostly been forgotten, and tourists who visit the cathedral take for granted that this is the final resting place of Davy Crockett.

Excavating remains from beneath the floor of San Fernando Cathedral.

The controversy started in 1889, when Colonel Juan Seguin wrote a letter stating that 50 years earlier he had taken the remains of the Alamo heroes and had buried them beneath the altar at San Fernando Cathedral. Most people dismissed the letter until almost 50 years later, when on July 28, 1936, workmen were digging a foundation for a new altar for the cathedral and they discovered charred human remains. Excitement grew as church officials realized the importance of the discovery. The remains were exhumed with a variety of witnesses on hand, including writer Frederick C. Chabot, Mayor C. K. Quin, Postmaster D. J. Quill, Adina DeZavala, granddaughter of Lorenzo DeZavala, and Mrs Leita Small, caretaker of the Alamo. The remains were placed on public display for a year, then entombed on May 11, 1938. To quell the rumors surrounding the findings, the diocese published a now rare book entitled *The Truth About the Burial of the Remains of the Alamo Heroes*.

However, today some still question whether Davy Crockett is actually buried there. Most likely he is not. First of all, Santa Anna ordered the cremation of all the bodies left at the Alamo. Most likely, Mexican and Texan soldiers were buried together. Secondly, Seguin did not return to the Alamo until after the Battle of San Jacinto, almost a month later. There is an excellent argument that the remains are those of the defenders of the Alamo; nevertheless, it would be a bit presumptuous to assume that they are the actual remains of Davy Crockett.

The Alamo Cenotaph

Situated on the north side of Alamo Plaza, the Alamo Cenotaph has received worldwide acclaim. Following the definition, the cenotaph honors the fallen heroes of the Alamo whose remains are elsewhere. The monument has a base made of Texas pink granite and a shaft constructed of Georgia gray marble that rises sixty feet. The cenotaph cost $100,000. The theme of the work is "The Spirit of Sacrifice," represented on the south and north side by the feminine figure, who also symbolizes Texas and the United States. On the east and west sides are the depictions of James Bowie, James Bonham, Davy Crockett, and William Travis, who represent all who died during the battle.

The cenotaph was the creation of renowned Italian sculptor Pompeo Coppini. Coppini was born in Italy and studied at the Academia Di Belle Arti in Florence. The sculptor moved to America in 1896 and became a naturalized American citizen in 1902. He eventually established a home and a studio in San Antonio because it reminded him of the terrain of his native Tuscany. Throughout his lifetime, he created monuments all over Texas, such as the five statues that comprise the Confederate Monument on the grounds of the state capitol.

Other works include a statue of President Rufus C. Burleson, president of Baylor University, the monument at Sam Houston's tomb in Huntsville, a memorial to Governor Sul Ross at Texas A&M, and the Texas Heroes Memorial in Gonzales. Coppini headed the art department at Trinity from 1942 until 1945, when he moved to New York. Coppini died in 1957 and was buried in San Antonio.

The Quadrangle and Geronimo

One of the most unusual places in San Antonio is the Quadrangle. The oldest building at Fort Sam Houston, it is now the headquarters to the Fifth U.S. Army. While many military installations discourage visitors with barbed wire and guards, the Quadrangle is just the opposite. Visitors are not only allowed, they are encouraged. As you step inside the stone walls, you immediately discover the perfect place for families to gather. Inside the fortress, deer, ducks, rabbits, and other small animals run free, as do the thousands of children who visit there every year. How did the headquarters for one of the world's most powerful armies become a petting zoo? Nobody seems to know.

The Quadrangle was built between 1876 and 1879. Before that, the U.S. Army used a variety of buildings in downtown San Antonio to house its officers, troops, and supplies. An arsenal (now the H.E.B. headquarters) was one of the few structures the U.S. Army owned. They used the Alamo for a Quartermaster depot and housed officers in the old Vance House (now the site of the Gunter Hotel). The Army was looking for a permanent site to call its own, and the city offered land at the head of Leon Springs. The Army rejected this because it was low-lying and susceptible to Indian raids. Most of the good land (land that had some height advantage) was in the hands of private citizens. When the headquarters for the local troops was relocated to Austin, city fathers recognized a need to offer a package of decent land or risk losing the military.

The land on the eastern part of the city became known as Government Hill. The Quadrangle was built without any outside windows or doors (except for the main gate) to provide for protection in case of attack. Two water towers were placed in the compound, as was a clock tower. The bell inside the clock tower was taken from a gunboat that had been grounded in Galveston Bay. It later hung in the Alamo when the U.S. Army used it as a depot. The clock was installed in 1882 by Bell and Brothers. The clock tower is unusual because a plaque commemorating the building of the Quadrangle is placed at the top where nobody can read it. It states:

San Antonio Quartermaster Depot
Erected by an Act of Congress - 1876
IN PEACE PREPARE FOR WAR

On September 10, 1886, the Quadrangle had perhaps its most famous visitor, Apache Indian Chief Geronimo. Geronimo had been leading the Indians in Arizona and New Mexico in skirmishes against the U.S. Army. The battles were quite brutal and many died on both sides. According to post records, a Lieutenant Gatewood convinced Geronimo to surrender. The chief and thirty other Apaches were escorted by Captain H. M. Lawton on a special train from Bowie, Arizona, to San Antonio.

While inside the walls, Geronimo was promised the protection of the U.S. Army. Tents were set up to serve as a shelter during their internment. The braves remained in San Antonio until October 22, when they were taken to Fort Pickens, Florida, and confined to an island ten miles off the coast of Florida. There are many stories connected with the chief's stay. One is that the deer in the Quadrangle were brought in for food for the 31 Indians. Another is that the Apaches were taken to the Lone Star Brewery and given a tour where they sampled the beer.

The Quadrangle has changed substantially since then. Windows were added to the outside, the water towers were removed, and the purpose of the structure was changed. On July 30, 1974, the complex was added to the National Register of Historic Places. As for the animals, no one is quite sure why they were added. Legend has it that Geronimo refused to eat army food, and the wild animals were added for his benefit. One thing is known—the deer and all the other animals have been there for over 100 years.

Members of Geronimo's tribe incarcerated at Fort Sam Houston's Quadrangle.

The Gift Chapel

One of the most interesting buildings in Fort Sam Houston is the post chapel, known better as the Gift Chapel. In 1907 Chaplain Thomas J. Dickson started a drive to raise money for a post chapel. Fort Sam had been without one since it opened in 1879. The church, located on Wilson Street two blocks east of New Braunfels Avenue, was built with $43,724 given to the post by the citizens of San Antonio in 1907. At the time, the army installation had outgrown its frontier image and was becoming more of a bustling army post. The need for a house of worship for the troops prompted the city's generosity.

On October 17, 1909, President William Taft dedicated the unfinished chapel. Also present at the dedication was presidential aide Captain Archibald Butt, who later died on the *Titanic*.

Over the years the church has slowly been finished. In 1930 a used pipe organ from an old war department theatre was installed. The chapel was completely remodeled in 1931 with light fixtures, a grand piano, the cross, and carpeting. Mamie Eisenhower donated money for a set of chimes in 1971 to commemorate her and her husband's association with the post. Some of the more striking features of the chapel are the flags which circle the main sanctuary. These were added in 1971. The Gift Chapel was entered in the National Register of Historic Places on May 17, 1974, and it is now one of five chapels of Fort Sam Houston.

Other Historic Notes on Fort Sam Houston

The National Historic Landmark: Over 500 acres and 932 buildings of Fort Sam Houston were designated a National Historic Landmark and Historic Conservation District in

1974. A marker designating the honor is displayed on Stanley Road just east of Reynolds Street.

Fort Sam Houston National Cemetery: The final resting place of thousands who served their country, the Fort Sam National Cemetery has some unusual features. Near the back of the grounds are the graves of Nazi, Japanese, and Italian soldiers from World War II. (The soldiers were POWs at Fort Sam.)

Also of interest is the number of soldiers who fought in the Spanish American War. Because of the length of the name of the war and the difficulty in carving tombstones during that era, the grave markers used an abbreviation. Instead of serving in the Spanish American War, thousands of veterans are remembered for serving in the SPAM War.

First Flight Memorial: Situated on the other side of Stanley Road, this memorial commemorates the first military flight made by Lieutenant Benjamin Foulois in 1910.

First WAAC Company: The first company of the Women's Army Auxiliary Corps was stationed at Fort Sam in 1942. Their barracks were located at the corner of Lawton and Patch. A historical marker now indicates the spot.

Camp Wilson Marker: In 1916 National Guard Troops were mobilized for border skirmishes with Pancho Villa in an area of the post known as Camp Wilson. A marker on Dickman Road between Reynolds and Allen indicates the site. Another camp, Camp Travis, was built shortly after to mobilize troops for World War I. Over 112,000 troops passed through the camp, which was located east of the New Braunfels Avenue and Stanley Road intersection. Of the 1400 buildings that once were part of Camp Travis, only three remain.

2nd Dragoons Stables: On Pine Street just south of Wilson is one of the Army's last mounted units. The ceremonial division welcomes visitors.

The Pershing House: The commanding general's quarters are named after Black Jack Pershing, who resided there in 1917. The home is one of the most striking on the post, if not in the entire city. It is located on Pershing Avenue just west of the Quadrangle.

Eisenhower Quarters: At the corner of Dickman and New Braunfels is the home that Colonel and Mrs. Eisenhower lived in when they were stationed at the post in 1941.

In 1916 a young Lieutenant Eisenhower lived at the BOQs at the corner of Grayson and New Braunfels across from the Quadrangle. These buildings were recently restored.

Infantry Post: At the end of Grayson Avenue is the grounds of the old Infantry Post. In service from 1885 to 1906, only a few buildings still exist from the old post. They include the BOQs at the corner of New Braunfels and Grayson, the old Officers' Mess across the street, the Commander's Quarters, and the Infantry Barracks. The post surrounded a parade field. Most of the area is now occupied by enlisted housing.

The Stilwell House: The commander's quarters for the old Infantry Post are named in honor of General Joseph W. "Vinegar Joe" Stilwell, who lived there from 1939 to 1940. Stilwell was commander of the U.S. troops in Burma during World War II.

Museums: Fort Sam Houston hosts two museums to assist visitors. The Fort Sam Houston Museum is open Wednesday through Sunday and is free. The U.S. Army Medical Department Museum is dedicated to military medical history and is open Wednesday through Sunday.

Read More About It:

Hardy, Mary Olivia. *History of Fort Sam Houston*. San Antonio: The Naylor Company, 1951.

Society for the Preservation of Historic Fort Sam Houston. *Guide to the Historic Homes at Fort Sam Houston*. San Antonio: 1989.

Turner, Leo. *The Story of Fort Sam Houston 1876-1936*. San Antonio: 1936.

Birthplace of the Air Force

Fort Sam Houston is widely recognized as a place of history. Eisenhower, Pershing, Geronimo, and MacArthur all spent time there. Fort Sam Houston is also recognized as the site of the first military flight and the birthplace of the Air Force.

Lieutenant Benjamin D. Foulois was serving at Fort Leavenworth when he first suggested that the Army consider using flying machines and balloons for military purposes. The suggestion was pretty much ignored until the Wright brothers offered the Army one of their wrecked airplanes. The Army decided to purchase the plane and sent for Foulois to come to San Antonio to repair and reassemble the plane and test it. The young lieutenant was perhaps the most qualified man in the Army to serve as its first pilot. He had taken a correspondence course in flying, he had flown with Wilbur Wright, and he was only 5 feet 5 inches tall and weighed 135 pounds (a small frame was essential for pilots in the early days of aviation).

It took almost a month for Foulois and his crew to repair the craft and make it airworthy. On March 2, 1910, at Arthur MacArthur Field (named for Douglas MacArthur's father who

Lt. Benjamin Foulois

15

was once the post commander), the Wright Flyer was catapulted into the air. The first military flight lasted seven minutes and reached the speed of fifty miles per hour. A crowd of 300 gathered on the outskirts of town to see the flight. The crowd later grew to thousands as a total of four flights were made that day.

The fourth flight ended in a slight mishap when a fuel line broke. The biplane dropped from the sky and the crash broke the plane's rudder. That ended the day's flying but was the beginning of aviation in the military. Foulois suggested two innovations that revolutionized transportation. One was to replace the catapult launching system with wheels for easier takeoffs and landings.

The second innovation was a result of the mishap on the fourth flight. Foulois was tossed around quite a bit. To prevent injury on his next flight, he took a leather strap from an old trunk and fashioned it into the world's first safety belt. The first military hangar was soon built in San Antonio, at the northeast end of the parade field.

Lt. Foulois spent the next four months setting world aviation distance and speed records. Tragedy struck May 10, 1911, when Lieutenant George E. M. Kelly was killed in a flying accident over Fort Sam. That ended military flights in San Antonio for three years. In 1915 Foulois was sent back to San Antonio to organize the first aero squadron. The unit was the first to see combat in the Pancho Villa skirmishes in Mexico.

Foulois served in World War I as chief of the air service. He retired in 1935 as a major general. He died April 25, 1967, two years before a man walked on the moon.

The Early Days of the Air Force

*"San Antonio is the hub of the largest aviation
center in the world"*
San Antonio Express   June 21, 1927

San Antonio was certainly a hub of activity during the early days of aviation. Because of its ideal weather conditions (it is said the city had only fifteen unsuitable flying days a year) and flat terrain, many early aviators came to San Antonio, including Katherine Stinson and Max Lillie.

U.S. Army biplanes flying in the U.S.A. formation over Randolph Field in 1935.

Benjamin Foulois conducted the first military flight at Fort Sam Houston in 1911 (see Birthplace of the Air Force), and soon planes flying over the city became a familiar sight. After a three-year ban of military flying due to safety concerns, the Army again opened Fort Sam to military flights. The War Department began to realize how useful aviation could be during wartime and soon was expanding the signal corps to include pilots. During the First World War, the Army asked for pilots to volunteer for service.

In 1917 Brooks Field and Kelly Field were opened to train Army aviators. Brooks became the home to the Army's primary flying school and also trained instructor pilots in the Gosport System of Flying (basically a tube that allowed the instructor to talk to his student while airborne). From 1919 to 1922 Brooks Field also became the home to the Army's Balloon Airship School. On Thanksgiving Day 1929 the first mass parachute drop was performed on the base, opening up another aspect to aviation warfare. Kelly Field was established as a school for advanced pilots, and for many years it was the Army's only base for such training. Some of the pilots who experienced early military flight training at the two bases include Charles Lindbergh, Billy Mitchell, Frank M. Hawk, Curtis Lemay, Claire Chennault, and Hap Arnold.

By 1926 Brooks and Kelly fields were no longer able to handle the number of pilots the Army wanted to train. The War Department wanted to open a new airfield but wanted the land free of cost. Cities from Shreveport to Dallas offered deals to bring the new military complex to their town. The Army wanted to stay in San Antonio, but the city had no land to offer. The city raised $500,000 through a confusing city ordinance (the first attempt to raise money for the land was ruled illegal) and, through German-speaking civic leaders who were dispatched to convince German farmers on the county's northeast corner to sell their land, were able to purchase the property. Randolph Field opened in 1930 and soon became known as the "West Point of the Air." The beautifully designed base was soon the pride of the Air

Corps. The large white water tower that dominates the facility was dubbed "Taj Mahal." From 1930 to 1939 Randolph Field was the nation's only primary and basic school for military pilots.

Randolph Field's contribution to the city would be far greater than anyone would have imagined. The military was becoming the city's major employer. Kelly Field's main mission shifted from pilot training to logistics. Soon the field was the largest employer in the city, hiring thousands of civil servants—many from the city's south side. Kelly Field's most important contribution was that it gave rise to a Hispanic middle class and forever changed the economic complexion of the city.

In 1946 a former bombing range for Kelly pilots became the San Antonio Aviation Cadet Center. Later named Lackland Air Force Base, this facility is the military's most widely known base. Because it is the Air Forces's only cadet training center, it's known as "the Gateway to the Air Force."

As for Brooks, its primary mission has shifted to medicine. In 1960 the base became home to the Aerospace Medical Division and the USAF School of Aerospace Medicine. The base is the second oldest active Air Force Base in the country. It was also the site of President Kennedy's last official act as Chief of State when he dedicated the opening of a new medical building there in 1963. The next day, he traveled to Dallas.

San Antonio may no longer be the hub of the world's largest aviation center but it is this country's premier military town, steeped in history and tradition.

Brothels

San Antonio was once the wildest frontier town in the West. The last civilized stop before heading west and the largest city in Texas, San Antonio at the turn of the century was a center for vice. From the Civil War until World War II, the city supported one of the most notorious red light districts in the country.

The sporting district was located in the southwest end of downtown, surrounded by Durango Street on the south, Santa Rosa on the east, Market Street on the north, and Frio on the west. The area is now mainly occupied by the elevated portion of I-35 and by a K Mart (prompting the historical joke that the red light has been replaced by the blue light).

The district grew into prominence after the Civil War. The area was frequented by soldiers on leave, East Coast businessmen who were visiting some of the area resorts, cowboys and cattlemen who were passing through the area, and area ranchers and farmers who were in town to market their goods. The area was also frequented by prominent local businessmen and politicians, along with average citizens from all walks of life.

The area was divided into three types of brothels: class A, B, and C. A class A brothel was by far the best. Located in fine mansions, many built by the same architects who built the homes in the King William district, these establishments were frequented by well-heeled patrons who would stay for about a week, sharing the company of one lady. These houses offered well-stocked bars, roulette wheels, crap tables, billiards, poker games, player pianos, velvet furniture coverings and drapes, along with brass rails and paintings of nudes. The patron would usually enjoy some gaming, dancing, and drinks before retiring for the evening.

The class B houses were usually upstairs in a saloon or a second class hotel. Finally, the class C sporting women worked out of "cribs," run down shacks that featured small rooms. The women would stand outside their small quarters and entice men on the street to sample their pleasures. The costs varied depending on the type of establishment you visited. A stop at a class A brothel would cost you one dollar, class B women charged fifty cents, and class C cribs cost a quarter (thus the derogatory phrase "a two-bit whore").

Visitors to the Alamo City learned quickly of the red light district from cab drivers and police, who were only too anxious to assist tourists to the sporting district and secure for themselves a generous tip. Perhaps the most unusual aspect of the brothel industry was The Blue Book, a directory of the area's houses. The book listed cab drivers who would take you into the district and a list of the ladies and madams who operated in the area. The 1911-1912 edition also listed the schedule for San Antonio's local baseball team and told where the area cock fights were held.

The Preface to the Blue Book stated:

> The Directory of the Sporting District is intended to be an accurate guide to those who are seeking a good time. To the stranger and visitor while in San Antonio, this book will be welcome, because it will put him on a proper and safe path as to where he may go and feel secure from hold ups and any other game usually practiced upon the stranger.
>
> Anyone perusing this booklet expecting to be regaled with lewd and obscene reading matter will be sadly disappointed: as outside of some harmless wit or toast, it contains only what necessary information is required to make it a directory.
>
> This Blue Book is at this writing the second one of its kind in the United States, (there being one in New Orleans, La.) and is issued strictly for information purposes, nothing else.

The red light district was run by a committee of brothel operators and saloon keepers. They set up rules of order in the area which were strictly enforced. They kept some semblance of peace in those rough and rowdy days. For many years the San Antonio Police Department was too small to enforce law and order in the area, and the control of the committee was appreciated.

The area finally died out during World War II. The Depression had severely hurt business and, when the dollars began to dry up, the control of the committee began to break down. Federal authorities, the I.R.S., and local moral leaders also chipped away at the once solid foundation of the sporting district. But the death blow came from perhaps the city's only industry bigger than vice: the military. During World War I, General Pershing thought prostitution was good for his troops; it helped keep morale up. However, during the second big war, parents who had heard stories of the wildness of San Antonio (and perhaps had visited the establishments themselves) pressured the Army into shutting down the district. The Army issued this threat, "Close down the brothels or we will place all of downtown S.A. off-limits to the soldiers."

Mayor Charles K. Quin, along with his police commissioner, flushed out the brothels, ran the women out, and put an end to one of the city's most notorious chapters. The district faded away and now only lives in the memory of old men who look back fondly on the days when San Antonio was a "sporting town."

"San Antonio is the wickedest city in the Union not exceeding Washington City which is the wickedest of hell."

December 7, 1885
Evangelist Dixie Williams
while preaching at a local Baptist Church

Brackenridge/Wheatley High School

At first there were two high schools. Brackenridge High was located at the corner of South St. Mary's and Temple, just south of downtown. It was named after George W. Brackenridge, who donated $40,000 for its construction in 1916. (Brackenridge, a notorious philanthropist, also donated the land for a park which bears his name.) The school colors were purple and white, and its mascot was the Eagle.

Wheatley High School was located at 415 Gabriel on the city's east side. It was originally a segregated black high school named after Phyllis A. Wheatley, an 18th century poet born in Africa and reared as a servant in Boston. The high school was built in the 1930s and replaced Douglass High School (named after the black abolitionist), which was located downtown. Interestingly, Douglass High School was built under the supervision of George Brackenridge and was made from stones that originally came from a Confederate building.

Wheatley High School's mascot was the Lion. But after 1970 the Lion roared no more. In 1969 a federal court order closed the predominantly black high school because it did not measure up to the standards of other schools in the San Antonio Independent School District. As part of the settlement with federal officials, school officials agreed to name the next new high school Wheatley High. The building housing the former Douglass High School became the home of Emerson Middle School and was designated a historic landmark.

Several sites for another Wheatley High School were proposed, but they were rejected for various reasons. They included expense of land acquisition, neighborhood make-up, physical site defects, and a location too far from the attendance area. The next new high school turned out to be the new version of Brackenridge built next to the old Brack building. School district officials decided the new building would be a marriage of the two old schools, adopting the name Wheatley and taking the school colors and mascot of Brackenridge.

This early 1970s solution met with opposition from both schools' students, graduates, and area residents. The debate and dissatisfaction of those involved raged for years. In late 1987 the debate resurfaced, and the San Antonio Independent School District decided that the new Wheatley High School would be renamed Brackenridge High and Emerson Middle School would become Wheatley Middle School.

A couple of footnotes in the Brackenridge/Wheatley controversy: George Brackenridge donated a lot of money not only to white schools but to black schools as well. According to his friend Alexander Terrell, his donations were a way of reconciling the fact that his parents owned two slaves prior to the Civil War. He donated money to Prairie View A&M, the now-defunct Guadalupe Colored College of Seguin, and an eastside school that bore his name.

The Good Government League

The Good Government League, or the GGL, was formed by local business and civic groups to help steer San Antonio in a political direction they deemed appropriate. The GGL was formed in December of 1954, with auto dealer Frank Gillespie, Sr., as its first president. The league was supposed to be a nonpartisan organization that would promote candidates who would best serve the interests of the entire city.

An executive committee ran the GGL and selected candidates it deemed appropriate for public office. One criterion was that the candidate must be wealthy so he could serve without pay. Candidates were also screened to ascertain that they were proponents of urban growth and economic expansion. In reality, a candidate was usually an upper-class member of the local power elite.

From 1955 to 1971 GGL candidates won seventy-seven of eighty-one city council races. Businessmen held the most power in the league, and through the use of the virtually hand-picked city council, they guided the future growth of the city. The Good Government League had a three-fold agenda: improve city services, prevent small municipalities from forming, and attract new businesses.

The first two goals were easily accomplished. Streets and drainage were vastly improved. A check of a city map will also show that there are few minor municipalities within the San Antonio city limits. However, attracting new business proved to be difficult. The city fathers worked the state legislature in order to lure a medical school and a branch of the University of Texas to the city in hopes of improving its business climate.

The demise of the Good Government League can be traced to a variety of causes. For one, the businessmen who ran the league split into two factions. One group wanted to concentrate on developing the north side; the other faction wanted to concentrate on downtown. The league, a victim of its own success, disintegrated over this issue.

Additionally, the rise of a middle-class Hispanic population (thanks to the vast employment opportunities at Kelly Air Force Base) gave growth to a new political power with its own agenda. The Hispanic population, especially those concentrated on the west side, felt neglected by the GGL. Their rising political power further hastened the demise of the fragmented league.

Perhaps the final nail in the coffin was the Justice Department's insistence that the city do away with its at-large council electorate system and adopt a district electorate system that would virtually guarantee minority representation. The 1977 newly elected city council had five Hispanics and one black, signifying the end of an era when the business community could dictate public policy.

The First Battle of Flowers

The Battle of Flowers parade is the oldest Fiesta event; it has survived two World Wars and a sniper attack. The annual Fiesta event, however, is very different from the first Battle of Flowers.

The year was 1891. Benjamin Harrison was president, and he was planning a trip to San Antonio on April 21. He was to make a speech on the anniversary of the Battle of San Jacinto. The people of San Antonio were quite thrilled that the president would be stopping in their city. No other president had ever been to San Antonio (for that matter, no pope had been here either). A parade and a "battle of flowers" were arranged in his honor. Unfortunately, it

An early Battle of Flowers float. Second boy from the left is noted architect Atlee B. Ayres in his younger days.

rained quite hard the day Harrison arrived, and the parade and flower battle were postponed until the inclement weather had passed. Three days later the rain was gone, but so was the president.

The parade, though, went on as originally planned. Floats and bicycles were decorated, and most of San Antonio's society people marched through the streets to Alamo Plaza. When they reached the plaza, the crowd split—half to the east and half to the west—to participate in a flower battle which was patterned after a similar event that was held in France (Nice and Cannes to be exact). At 6:20 P.M. on April 24, 1891, the two teams began to throw flowers at each other in a "battle" which lasted for forty minutes.

As the years passed, the "flower battle" was phased out, but the parade stayed and more events were added. In 1900 Fiesta became a week-long event. Today there are four parades, over one hundred events, and nine days of fun and merriment each Fiesta.

The Mexican Market

For many San Antonians, life without weekly trips to the H.E.B. would seem impossible. But one hundred years ago, Handy Andy was nothing more than a neighbor down the street who was useful with tools. The marketplace was where most of the shopping took place. The most colorful market was the Mexican Market. Much of the market still exists as El Mercado, but it is drastically different from the bustling shops that existed there previously. The Mexican Market consisted of many parts.

There was Haymarket Plaza, or the Haymarket. This majestic building stood on the corner of Commerce and San Saba. The farmer's market took place here, and for quite some time the chili queens were a part of the scene. The building that dominated Haymarket Plaza is now gone, replaced by a new building which serves as both a farmer's market and a parking lot. The Municipal Market House still stands at the corner of Santa Rosa and Commerce. In its heyday, it was the section of the market that specialized in meats and fresh cut flowers. Today the building is a main part of El Mercado but is used mainly as a place to sell souvenirs from Mexico. Produce Row, the walk that runs through the center of El Mercado, was aptly dubbed due to the abundance of fruits and vegetables sold there. Produce was also sold at Washington Square which is across Market Street. The open-air plaza where vendors hawked their wares is now occupied by a government building and a parking lot.

The Chili Queens

Before there were fast food restaurants, Pig Stands, or coffee shops, there were the chili queens. Originally, these women would serve chili and other Tex-Mex fare throughout the day to the cattle drivers, tourists, and city folks who would dine in open-air markets. At night when the farmers would pack their wares, the chili queens would multiply and would be accompanied by lanterns, music, and dancing. Most historians agree that the chili queens became a common sight in San Antonio some time in the late 1870s. Originally, they set up their tables and kettles at Military Plaza. In 1888 the city hall was built on that site, and the queens moved their trade to Alamo Plaza and Haymarket Plaza (where the farmer's market is now).

It can be argued that chili was unique to San Antonio and to the queens. The meat that was used to make the dish was tough and sinewy, much like beef was in the 1880s when cattle roamed free. Such a cut of beef was readily available in a major cattle town such as San Antonio and easily afforded by all. The queens would also serve up other Mexican dishes, which many believe are the forerunners of today's Tex-Mex cuisine.

San Antonio's chili queens had a reputation throughout the West. William Jennings Bryan dined in the open-air market. The 1893 World's Fair in Chicago featured a booth called San Antonio Chili Stand. One problem with the stands was their lack of sanitary standards. Nobody was quite sure of the actual ingredients. In 1900 a chili stand operator was put on trial for allegedly using horse meat. Maury Maverick writes in his book *A Maverick American* that many locals believed that pigeons, dogs, and other animals were occasional chili ingredients.

Chili Tables, Alamo Plaza, in front of the Postoffice, San Antonio, Texas.

Chili stands on Alamo Plaza in 1908.

As shoppers moved from open-air markets to super-markets and plazas were converted to parks, the chili queens were slowly forced to smaller parks, side streets, and back-yards where their numbers thinned. In 1943 the remaining chili queens disappeared when they were forced to obey the same health codes as restaurant operators. Once a year, during Night in Old San Antonio (NIOSA), the chili queens reappear complete with picnic tables, lanterns, and kettles. True to form, they are located in the back of La Villita in the Mexican Market area.

The Buckhorn Saloon

Few saloons have ever become as famous as the Buckhorn. During the wild West days, it was legendary. It was even immortalized in Larry McMurtry's Pulitzer Prize winning novel, *Lonesome Dove*. The bar still exists today, as a tourist attraction on the grounds of the Lone Star Brewery. But in its heyday, it was a unique part of San Antonio lore.

Opening in 1881, on Dolorosa Street, by Albert Friedrich, the bar immediately attracted trappers, cowboys, cattlemen, and traders who often traded horns for drinks. Soon the bar was filled with horns, and the legacy grew.

Bartenders at the famous Buckhorn.

In 1896 the Buckhorn moved to the corner of Houston and Soledad. Friedrich ran his bar with a no-nonsense approach. He prided himself on the fact that no man was ever killed in his bar. His customers respected the barkeep and his place of business. Gunholders were asked to check their weapons at the bar before being served. Many cowboys would check their wallet and their guns for safekeeping at the Buckhorn and retrieve them before they left town.

The Buckhorn was known for its vast horn collection which included a seventy-eight-point deer, as well as for a host of other oddities. Every election day was known as ladies' day at the bar. The bar would be closed, and men would not be allowed to enter unless accompanied by a woman. The Buckhorn also had very few chairs. Friedrich did not want his customers to linger.

In its later years, the Buckhorn became a familiar stomping ground for visiting military. It also became more of a curio shop. It seemed everybody wanted a souvenir from the world famous bar. In 1957 the Buckhorn and its now vast collection of horns was bought and moved to the Lone Star Brewery. A replica of the bar is open to customers; the original bar is located in the back. The collection of horns (and now fins and feathers) is now adequately displayed for all to see. The collection is said to include every type of horned animal in the world.

John "Bet-A-Million" Gates
and Barbed Wire

Until the 1870s, cattlemen throughout Texas let their cattle run free across the open plains. Large ranches were nonexistent. Because of the lack of wood and rocks on the Texas plains, ranchers had few materials with which to make fences, therefore making it too difficult to protect their property. But a young Illinois native changed the cattle business forever on one fateful day.

John Gates, 22 and just out of college, came to San Antonio to peddle an unusual product, barbed wire. Gates claimed that the wire was stronger than whiskey and cheaper than dirt, and there wasn't a steer that could get through it. The cowboys were skeptical, to say the least. With so many cattlemen passing through town on their great trail drives to Kansas City, Gates could not find any customers. So the young salesman organized a demonstration on Military Plaza. He convinced city officials to let him construct a corral on the plaza. Afterwards, he invited cowboys to bring their longhorns into the enclosure and watch as the unusual fence tamed the wildest steer. The fence and the demonstration worked so well that Gates sold a boxcar full of wire that night.

That year three million pounds of wire were sold. The next year sales more than quadrupled. By 1880 eighty million pounds were sold, and the cattle business was changed forever. The open range disappeared as landowners fenced off their land to protect their watering grounds and cattle. Cattle drives were replaced by trains which were spreading coast to coast. The longhorn lost out to the fine beef cattle. By 1884 cutting a barbed wire fence was a felony.

As for John Gates, he formed his own barbed wire company and made a fortune. The flamboyant wheeler-dealer picked up the name Bet-A-Million and later played a role in the oil boom that hit in 1901. The spot on Military Plaza where the now famous demonstration took place is currently occupied by city hall. A historical marker commemorating the event now stands there.

The Camels Come to San Antonio

On June 18, 1856, the people of San Antonio viewed one of the most unusual sights of their lifetime—a troop of army camels marching through the streets of downtown! Thus began the camel's brief history with the Army. Secretary of War Jefferson Davis sponsored an experiment to use the desert creatures as a pack animal. At the time, the Army relied heavily on the mule to transport supplies. Many in the War Department felt camels would better suit the Army in the wide open spaces of the American Southwest.

Camels could move faster than mules. They did not have to follow routes that had water because of their ability to store great amounts of the liquid. They could travel better through mud and could carry heavier loads with less upkeep and less equipment than could mules.

In May of 1856 thirty-four camels arrived in Indianola and began marching toward San Antonio, led by Brevet Major Henry C. Wayne. On June 18 they arrived in the city and camped at San Pedro Springs where the camels rested and refueled. The beasts of burden stayed only a short time before moving on to Camp Verde, an experimental outpost near Kerrville, where they spent the rest of their lives.

Although the new pack animals passed all their tests, they never caught on with the Army. The horses that the military used became unruly around the camels, most likely due to their odd appearance or their offensive odor. But mainly the camels were a victim of poor public relations. Despite their excellent performance, the people who occupied the Southwest disliked the camels and preferred to stick with the more familiar horse and mule.

The Pope Comes to San Antonio

On September 13, 1987, the eyes of the world focused on San Antonio when Pope John Paul II visited the Alamo City. This was the Pope's second visit to the United States. He began in Miami, then went to Columbia, South Carolina, and New Orleans before stopping in San Antonio. The pontiff ended his tour by visiting Phoenix, Los Angeles, Monterey (California), San Francisco, and Detroit.

Months of planning went into the visit. A mass site to accommodate 500,000 worshipers was chosen in the then-undeveloped area of Westover Hills. Security, transportation, medical and sanitary concerns for a half million visitors took months of careful planning. Two events before the visit helped scar a near-perfect day. First, an overly cautious public health official expressed her concerns to the local media that hundreds would die at the papal mass site. Fortunately, her fears were unfounded; nevertheless, safety concerns kept the expected crowd of 500,000 to a more manageable 350,000.

The altar at the mass became a newsworthy item when, a few days before the event, heavy winds toppled two towers that framed the stage. There was little time to rebuild the towers, so cranes were brought in to support the remaining backdrop.

Those hoping to capitalize on the Pope's visit ended up disappointed. Despite the hundreds of thousands of visitors that flocked to the city, the worshipers chose not to buy papal lawn sprinklers (dubbed "Let us Spray"), paper papal hats, "popesicles," and other cheap souvenirs that could be found on every street corner. In spite of an early rush on accommodations, most hotels experienced a supply of empty rooms. Many pilgrims stayed with host families that volunteered their homes through local churches of every denomination. Hundreds of lodging reservations were left unused when the size of the crowd became a worry.

The Pope arrived at Kelly Air Force Base at 10:00 A.M., Sunday, September 13, 1987. His motorcade took him to the mass site, where he immediately toured the grounds allowing the throngs to get an up-close look at the leader of the Catholic church. Pope John Paul delivered a sermon in both English and Spanish and saluted those who worked "on behalf of suffering brothers and sisters arriving from Latin America." Thousands received communion with the help of hundreds of laymen. The stifling heat, which caused so much concern to public health officials, was not a problem for the pontiff. Despite wearing heavy robes and a miter, he stayed cool, thanks to a specially designed chair with air conditioning vents.

After the mass the Pope traveled to Assumption Seminary where he had lunch with the Bishops of Texas. His motorcade paraded to the Municipal Auditorium at 4:00, allowing thousands more to view him. At 4:30 he spoke to Catholic Charities USA at the auditorium; then, he went on to San Fernando Cathedral where he addressed students preparing to enter the priesthood.

One of his most inspirational stops was at Plaza Guadalupe at a westside barrio, one of the poorest sections of the city. John Paul spoke on the importance of parish life. He ended his day at Assumption Seminary where a delegation of Polish Americans from Panna Maria met with the first Polish pope.

The visit was extensively covered by all three network affiliated television stations. Without a doubt, the visit of Pope John Paul II touched every person in San Antonio in some way.

The Chapel of the Miracles

While driving into downtown from the north side via I-10, motorists may notice a small chapel near the San Antonio Independent School District Food Processing Plant. This small, unsanctioned, privately owned church is one of the city's oldest religious institutions, the Chapel of the Miracles, or El Capilla de Miragolas. Once a thriving area, the land around the small church has been cleared in the name of urban renewal, and only the chapel has been spared.

Built in the early 1870s by a Canary Islander, beside San Pedro Creek, the chapel has long been the destination of those seeking miracles. The crucifix, known as El Senor de los Milagros, is believed to have come from San Fernando Cathedral after a fire in 1813. The crucifix is said to have originally come from Spain and was brought over to be housed in Mission de Valero, which was originally on the same site as the chapel. Over the years the blind, deaf, and crippled have claimed to have been cured by this crucifix, which is believed to be over 400 years old.

The chapel is only thirty feet by forty feet, but its small size means little to the numbers of people who believe in its powers. The chapel sits on Solado Street off the I-10 access road and is open from 9 to 4 daily.

Communist Encounter I

The American South was never a fertile ground for the communist movement. During the 1930s communism was a new concept embraced by many labor leaders and liberal intellectuals, but in the South, where even labor unions were frowned upon, the communist movement never gained a foothold.

The exception was San Antonio. With its large population of Mexican Americans who lived in poverty, the city proved to be a fertile ground for communist agitators. Most of the Hispanics who lived in San Antonio worked for $1.50 a week shelling pecans. After the minimum wage law of 25 cents an hour was put into effect in 1939, thousands of pecan shellers were replaced by machines.

A young lady named Emma Tenayuca was appalled by the poverty of the west side. Standing only 5 feet 1 ½ inches tall, she grew up in comparatively comfortable conditions on the city's west side. By the time she graduated from Brackenridge High School, she had denounced the Catholic church and become a communist. In 1932 she began organizing strikes and soon took over the local chapter of the Worker's Alliance. Throughout the west side, she was known as La Pasionaria after the communist passion flower of the Spanish Civil War. For her efforts, she was arrested twice, and her local headquarters were often trashed by the police. Her followers once took over city hall, and on another occasion they organized a sit-down at the police station. Despite all that, few took her seriously, and she was considered more of a nuisance than a threat.

In 1937 Tenayuca married Homer Brooks, of Houston, who had once run for governor on the Communist Party ticket. She also traveled to New York, where she met with the leaders of the American Communist movement. In August of 1939, in an effort to impress her East Coast conteporaries, she wrote a two-sentence letter to the mayor requesting use of Municipal Auditorium for a communist rally. Mayor Maury Maverick, a staunch defender of the Bill of Rights, an attorney for the American Civil Liberties Union, and a former New Deal congressman, granted a permit for the rally, fully realizing that he might also be signing away his political career.

Emma Tenayuca leading a workers rally on the steps of city hall.

A week before the gathering, it was revealed that Russia had signed a nonaggression pact with Nazi Germany. Americans believed they would soon be pulled into World War II, and the actions of Russia caused anticommunist sentiment to swell. The timing of the rally could not have been worse. Various church and veteran groups protested the permit, but the mayor refused to revoke it. Many were appalled that the Municipal Auditorium, which was dedicated to those who served in World War I, was to be used by communists.

On the day of the rally, a poster of Joseph Stalin was hung inside the hall. Even though the mayor believed that the meeting would take place without incident, he had most of the police on hand just in case. His prudence proved to be justified. Despite the fact that only 100 people showed to attend the rally, 5,000 showed up to protest. The mayor could hear the angry crowd from his home two miles away.

The mob threw stones and burned Maverick in effigy. Ignoring tear gas and water hoses, they rushed the auditorium. Tenayuca and her followers escaped with police escort via the basement. When the horde entered the auditorium, they proceeded to break every window in the place and slash all the seats. Firehoses were cut, and the rioters held their own victory rally inside. Fourteen police officers and a host of protesters were injured in the melee.

The events of August 25 had many aftereffects. Emma Tenayuca, the young, petite communist leader, was never heard from again. As for the city of San Antonio, it had suffered its most disgraceful moment, with the eyes of the nation watching. Conservative and liberal newspapers alike condemned the mob action, and one national magazine, the *Forum and Century*, labeled San Antonio "The Shame of Texas."

As for Maury Maverick, his career as mayor would soon be over. His many accomplishments (such as the restoration of La Villita) and his years as a U.S. Congressman meant little to the electorate who dumped him the next year. For years he was remembered simply as "the guy who let the commies use the auditorium." A popular story that circulated throughout the city afterward had Maverick leaving a church service where a prominent woman cornered him and said, "I hear all over town you're a communist. But if you come to church you can't be a communist." To which Maverick reportedly replied, "I hear all over town that you're a whore, but I didn't believe them either."

Communist Encounter II

March 20, 1980, is a day that will not be forgotten by right-wing haters of godless communists. For on that day, the red wave hit San Antonio like it had never been hit before. Communists took over the cradle of Texas liberty—the Alamo.

Early that spring afternoon, Abigail Buyers, Damien Garcia, and Haydan Fisher, members of the Revolutionary May Day Brigade of the Maoist Revolutionary Communist Party, scaled the outer wall of the Alamo. They promptly lowered the Texas flag and raised a red flag. Perched atop the shrine for thirty minutes, they shouted slogans and had other members of their group hand out leaflets. The leftists urged the crowd that had gathered to join them in a May 1st protest against the oppression of Hispanics.

The police were swift and quickly removed the trio from atop the Alamo. No weapons were found among the three, who were taken downtown and charged with desecrating a venerated object. Supporters posted bond, and they were quickly released. The charge was later reduced to disorderly conduct.

One of the trespassers never returned to San Antonio to stand trial. Damien Garcia was stabbed in Los Angeles and died a month before the trial.

Though the Alamo was once again safe from communism, it was not free of shame. For the next few years, the Ku Klux Klan took it upon themselves to protect the Alamo on May Day.

Finck Cigars and the Travis Club

In the late 19th century, cigar making was a popular Texas industry, especially among the newly arrived Germans. Freidrich Ernest, the father of German immigration in Texas, was himself a cigar maker. Only one cigar maker remains today, the Finck Cigar Company of San Antonio. When H. W. Finck, a second-generation German American, set up shop in San Antonio, the city was already home to 18 other manufacturers. At the time, most American cities had a handful of cigar manufacturers, most being one-man operations. The Finck family lived upstairs from their small business, which later moved to a small factory located just west of Martin Street. The Finck's ability to adapt to a changing industry is one reason the company was able to survive.

In 1910 Finck made a special cigar for members of the Travis Club. The Travis Club was an elite social club for prominent San Antonians, with a multistoried building downtown for its clubhouse. The cigar was for members of the Travis Club only. During World War I, the club opened its doors to servicemen, who made it a popular hangout—so popular, in fact, that there was little room left for the members. After the war, the members failed to return and the club folded. However, the Travis Club cigar lived on. The company was flooded with orders from servicemen who had sampled the smoke during their stay in San Antonio. Thus began the Travis Club brand. As for the beautiful building featured on the box, it has been torn down.

Today the company is still going strong, as is the Travis Club line of cigars which can be purchased today by the general public. Finck Cigars are only sold in Texas and through special orders. The company boasts that it uses 100% tobacco as compared to a homogenized blend. The Fincks, now in their fourth generation of cigar manufacturers, are the last of a breed. Their factory at 414 Vera Cruz is the last in Texas.

Henry William Finck's membership certificate to the Travis Club.

The Corn Chip in San Antonio

Any true connoisseur of that fried cornmeal snack treat known simply as the Frito will surely know the legend of its origin. As the story goes, Elmer Doolin, future founder of the Frito-Lay company, was in San Antonio in the early 1930s. While dining at a small Mexican restaurant in San Antonio, Doolin became fascinated with a chip which could be purchased with lunch. He discovered the Mexican national who created the recipe and paid him one hundred dollars for it, allowing the man to return home to Mexico. He then took the recipe back to Dallas, where he eventually turned it into a snack food fortune.

According to the Frito-Lay company, Elmer Doolin owned an ice cream business that was in the middle of a price war, and he was looking for another investment. One afternoon in September of 1932, while waiting for a nickel sandwich at a local lunch stop, he noticed a small package that contained an interesting treat for five cents. Inside he found a fried corn snack treat. He sought out the maker and bought the recipe, nineteen retail accounts, and an old converted hand-operated potato ricer used for making the Fritos, for $100. Some sources say that Doolin borrowed the money from his mother, who had to pawn her wedding ring. Doolin manufactured the Fritos at night in his mother's kitchen on Roosevelt Street, producing ten pounds of chips an hour. The young businessman sold the chips from his Ford Model T and earned about two dollars a day. In 1933 the Frito company expanded and moved to Dallas.

The man who is credited with bringing masa, the corn-meal used in Fritos, to Texas is Bartolo Martinez. Martinez learned to make masa in Yucatan and moved to San Antonio in 1896 to begin marketing in the U.S. Martinez built a number of masa mills around San Antonio. The first large-scale plant to grind meal into masa was built in 1903, at the corner of San Fernando and Leona. Eighty-three years later, the Martinez Mill and Factory was set for restoration when a two-alarm fire struck the old wooden structure at 5:22 P.M. on July 26, 1986. The structure, located at 701 Leona Street, was listed as a national landmark by the National Register of Historic Places. The dilapidated building sat in the middle of the Vista Verde South redevelopment area and had recently been purchased by the San Antonio Development Agency. Arson was suspected.

Interestingly enough, many Mexican restaurants in the Dallas-Ft. Worth area still serve freshly made Frito-style chips with their dinners, while in San Antonio the fried tortilla chip is in vogue.

The KMAC Clock

KMAC was a radio station that existed in San Antonio until the early 1980s (the station was at 630 kHz, now KSLR AM). Though the station no longer exists, San Antonians are reminded of its past with the KMAC clocks. According to Joe Anthony, formerly of KMAC radio and the self-professed "godfather of rock and roll," the clocks were part of a radio promotion from 1956 to 1958. The green neon clocks were given as a bonus to businesses which bought 32 one-minute commercials for 250 dollars.

Many businesses around San Antonio still have their clocks prominently displayed. Among the businesses displaying the clocks are the Nix Hospital parking garage, the Winn's in Alamo Heights, and Dailey's Liquor on San Pedro. Most establishments report that they have never owned a timepiece that kept better time. Though most have received offers for their clocks that exceed their original investment, few have parted with them.

Other locations spotted with KMAC clocks:
    Duke Electric; corner of Sixth and Ave E
    Johnson Beauty College; 402 Travis
    Northside Pharmacy; 5607 San Pedro

The Flower Shop in the Gas Station Bathroom

At the corner of Broadway and Austin Highway was once a small flower shop, The Blooming Basket. What is so unusual about this small store is that it was located in what was formerly the ladies' room of a Mobil gas station.

The Mobil station at that corner was a throw-back to the days of 30-cents-a-gallon gasoline and full service. When it was built, it was at the edge of town, one of the last places to fill up before a long trip to Austin (hence the name Austin Highway). The ladies' room was more than a place to take care of life's necessities, it was a place to relax and refresh oneself before an arduous journey. The ladies' room had wicker furniture, a tile floor, artwork, draperies, and a fireplace. Many stories on the oddity of such a luxurious gas station bathroom were reported in the local media. The extravagant facilities survived into the 1980s. Unfortunately, the men's room was your basic filling station restroom.

When the gas station closed in the mid-1980s, many felt a loss. The red Mobil Pegasus atop the station became the property of the San Antonio Conservation Society. The ladies' room with its ample space became a flower shop. Later, the flower shop moved to larger quarters, and the entire gas station was redeveloped. The ladies' room has been neatly redesigned to add more floor space to the building. Only the sign outside a now unused door reminds motorists of what was arguably the nicest gas station bathroom in Texas.

The Case of the Missing Sculpture

Throughout the history of modern art, many people have mistaken these works as junk, not art. Such was the case of Asteriskos II, a 3-ton black metal sculpture which the Catto family commissioned from Tony Smith, a New York sculptor, for Hemisfair. Its original location was between the Arena and the Convention Center.

After the fair closed, the huge work disappeared. It took over a year for the piece to be found. Unfortunately, it was no longer intact. It seems the artwork was carted off, only to be later blow-torched into smaller pieces, fitted with wooden lids, and turned into tool boxes and ice chests for after-work beer parties at the Zarzamora St. Public Works Department yard.

The Catto family commissioned a replica from the artist and donated it to the McNay Art Institute where it sits today.

Wings - The Movie

The first movie to win the Oscar for best picture has its roots in the Alamo City. The silent World War I epic *Wings* was filmed in San Antonio, using its many military facilities as backdrops. Kelly and Brooks fields were used as cadet training sites. The Ft. Sam Houston gate near the Quadrangle was used in the opening shot, and Camp Stanley acted as St. Mihiel, France, where the 2nd Infantry fought.

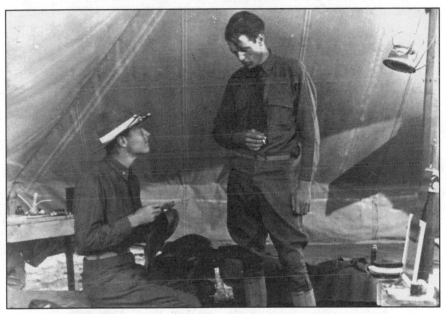

Actors Richard Arlen and Gary Cooper (right) in a scene from the movie Wings, *filmed in San Antonio.*

The film premiered in San Antonio on May 19, 1927, at the Texas Theatre (see Old Theatres). Proceeds from the event ($5,500) were given to a memorial fund for the 2nd Infantry Division, which lost 25,000 troops in World War I.

Actors Buddy Rogers, Clara Bow, Richard Arlen, and Jobyna Ralston attended the premier of their film, as did many actors from the movie *Rough Riders* which was filming in San Antonio at the time.

The movie also featured the screen debut of Gary Cooper who was on screen for a total of 102 seconds. Cooper received such a reaction from fans who wrote the studio asking about the tall actor that his fate as a star was born.

The premiere ended on a spectacular note, when moviegoers left the theatre and were greeted by newsboys who were selling papers announcing that former Brooks Field Cadet Charles Lindbergh was preparing to leave for Paris on his solo transatlantic flight.

The Last Humble Station

Before there was Exxon, there was Esso. And, in Texas, there was Humble Oil. Humble Oil was once the most important oil company in Texas with service stations stretched across the state and huge refineries that supplied both Texans and motorists across the country. But all the Humble stations have disappeared from the Texas landscape. On December 1, 1959, Standard Oil of New Jersey bought controlling interest in Humble and took over. In 1972 the Humble name was replaced by a new moniker, Exxon. Some of the old Humble stations have been abandoned, others have been remodeled with a new corporate logo affixed above the station. All the Humble stations are gone. All but one.

The last Humble station no longer pumps gas, and it has no employees. As a matter of fact, it doesn't even have windows. It's been closed for years. The last Humble station still has its sign, though. An interesting mosaic on the side of the building marks it permanently as an outpost for Humble Oil.

The building is located just south of downtown (take the South Alamo exit off I-10 and travel north just past the post office). Bypassed by thousands of cars daily, it exists in a void. Too small for redevelopment, but saved from demolition by being far enough away from the highway, the station sits empty as a monument to the past.

The Term "Maverick"

The *American Heritage Dictionary* defines "maverick" as
1. An unbranded or orphaned range animal, especially a calf. 2a. a nonconformist 2b. an independent as in politics.

It lists as the origin of the word Samuel A. Maverick, Texas cattleman. Maverick was a signer of the Texas Declaration of Independence, an Alamo defender, and a prominent San Antonian—but he was hardly a Texas cattleman. According to Texas legend, Samuel Maverick was a cattleman of mammoth proportions. He owned mighty ranches and sent thousands of cattle to market every year. Maverick let his cattle roam free on the plain, unbranded. Whenever a cowboy came across an unbranded cow he'd exclaim, "That's

Samuel Maverick on his 90th birthday.

Maverick's cow." Shortly, any unbranded cattle became known simply as a maverick. The term was passed around the West and evolved to mean anybody who was an unbranded character.

According to Maury Maverick, Samuel's grandson, his grandfather was never a cattle baron. In his book *A Maverick American*, Maury Maverick writes that the legend began in 1845 when Samuel Maverick had 400 head of cattle. He left the cattle to the care of a man who never bothered to brand the herd. Maverick put the cattle on a peninsula, but the water was so shallow the herd would wander across to the mainland. The caretaker, Jack, never paid much attention to the job and let them wander freely. The small herd only got larger in legend and were finally branded and sold in 1853. The legend of Maverick the so-called cattle baron was pushed west in 1849 by California Gold Rushers who landed on the Texas coast and pushed their way west from there.

Samuel Maverick was surely an heroic Texan, but a cattle baron? That is little more than a Texas tall tale.

Yes Virginia, There was an Alligator in the San Antonio River

San Antonio is not a natural habitat for alligators, so stories of alligator sightings in local waterways are usually dismissed as urban legends. But . . . the San Antonio River once hosted an alligator. It's true, it's true.

On Saturday, November 4, 1989, Texas Wildlife officials were alerted to the presence of an alligator near Espada Dam. Sunday morning, the fifth of November, game officials searched the river once in the morning and again in the afternoon. With the help of local fisherman and a casting net, state game warden Denny Villalobos pulled a three-foot alligator from the river. State officials speculated that the alligator was either dropped into the river by someone who originally thought of the creature as a pet, or that the animal migrated north when its water hole evaporated.

A month earlier, a seven-foot alligator was retrieved from Medina Lake after two weeks of sightings. That reptile was killed with a blow to the head, possibly from a motorboat.

Sam, the Space Monkey

Sam was the first Texan to travel into space. Born in 1957 at the University of Texas, Sam, a rhesus monkey, was designated for the U.S. space program because he was a stand-out at the U.T. Balcones Research Center. On December 4, 1959, Sam was launched into space from Wallops Island, Virginia. After a seventeen-hour countdown, Sam was launched fifty-five miles into space and spent a total of twelve minutes there.

After his famous flight, Sam was brought to the School of Aerospace Medicine at Brooks Air Force Base, where he was put under medical scrutiny. The space chimp made the cover of *Parade* magazine in 1960, but his fame was short-lived when John Glenn became more popular.

Sam was kept at Brooks AFB for a mere eleven years when the Air Force figured they had gathered enough evidence on the effects of twelve minutes of space flight on monkeys. Sam then moved to a cage at the San Antonio Zoo where he was given a companion, though he was now too fat to mate. A plaque on his cage told zoo goers of the accomplishments of Sam.

The space pioneer passed away on September 19, 1978. The chimp's body was taken back to Brooks for an autopsy, where more was learned of the effects of weightlessness.

SECTION II

SAN ANTONIO PEOPLE

Germans in San Antonio

Despite its prominent Hispanic population, historians look at old San Antonio as a town with a mostly German influence. Approximately 30,000 German immigrants came to South Texas before the Civil War. Books and magazines on Texas were widely circulated throughout the area of the lower Rhine in Germany, making this portion of North America very popular overseas. Dozens of German villages sprung up throughout the area. Henri Castro established a settlement of Alsatians on the Medina River which became Castroville. German influences still ring out in New Braunfels, Fredricksburg, and other hill country towns.

Immigrant Germans had a profound effect on San Antonio. Most were Roman Catholic and tended to settle southwest of the river along the Alamo Ditch (the Acequia Madre) in an area that became known as "the Little Rhine."

The new San Antonians never assimilated into southern life; instead, they recreated their European culture right in San Antonio. A German-English school located on South Alamo was created in 1859. It was dedicated to Friedrich Schiller with the purpose of educating the children of German intellectuals. The school had two main principles: one was that religious instruction would be prohibited at the school; the other was that German and English should be given the same amount of instruction. The school drew students from throughout Texas and was recognized as one of the outstanding cultural institutions of 19th century Texas. The building, constructed by John Kampmann, still stands today.

One of the first newspapers in San Antonio was a German language press, the *San Antonio Zeitung*, established in 1848.

For years the focal point of German culture was the Casino Club, built on Market Street in 1857. For a generation, it was restricted to ethnic Germans and to U.S. Army officers (Robert E. Lee spent off-duty time there). The club's patrons were highly interested in the arts and sponsored many operas and other performing arts productions. The membership consisted mainly of prominent local businessmen and well-heeled Germans who conversed in German while at the club (German being the official language).

German businesses and churches also began to spring up throughout San Antonio. St. Joseph's Catholic Church and Academy was established in 1867 on Commerce Street. Across from La Villita Street, St. John's Lutheran Church was formed. Menger, Friedrich, Oppenheimer, Groos, Geunther, and Joske are just a few German family names that became associated with prominent local businesses.

After the Civil War, German prominence began to increase. The German community as a whole was mainly pro-Union and antislavery. Many Germans lived in frontier towns and feared secession because it would mean the end of the federal government's intervention in Indian problems. Small German farmers had little use for slaves, and most Texas Germans wished that slavery would be abolished, but they felt the states had the right to decide. Because of its location (west of the main fighting) and its disposition (mainly pro-Union), San Antonio rebounded quickly from the Civil War. German merchants made good money from the cattlemen who came through the city after the conflict. Fortunes increased even more when the railroad came to town. By this time, the big money cattle kings had disappeared, but the German locals were now into their second generation.

Prominent German-Americans built the King William neighborhood. Named for King Wilhelm I of Prussia, who later became German emperor, the neighborhood was established as a showplace of stately German homes. The area, built on the old agricultural grounds of the Valero mission, was planned by Ernst Hermann Altgelt (who founded Comfort, Texas). Many homes had magnificent gardens irrigated with water from the old acequias. The neighborhood originally was to run for miles, but ended after a few blocks when Carl Geunther built his Pioneer Flour Mills. For more than a generation, King William, sometimes referred to as "Sauerkraut Bend," was the best address in town.

German culture continued to flourish in the latter part of the 19th century. The San Antonio Turn Verein, a gymnastic troupe, performed regularly on Bowen's Island. The troupe also built a variety of halls for their organization. The first one was built next to the Menger and was incorporated into the hotel when the Menger expanded in 1875. The troupe's second building was located at the southeast corner of Houston and St. Mary's streets. Its final home was built in 1901 on Bonham Street. The beautiful structure still exists as the Bonham Exchange night club. The Turn Verein were also responsible for the first volunteer fire department in San Antonio.

An association dedicated to German classical music was also formed, and they built the Beethoven Maennerchor, the finest concert hall in the Southwest, in 1895 on South Alamo Street. The hall burnt down in 1913 and was immediately rebuilt. The building lost its facade during the widening of Alamo Street. The once-grand building fell into further disgrace when the KKK used it as a meeting place in 1924. The concert hall, located on the southwest corner of Alamo Plaza, is now owned by the city. There was once talk of rebuilding the original facade during Hemisfair redevelopment negotiations, but that proposal has been dropped.

A fraternal lodge, the Sons of Herman, was also organized in San Antonio on July 6, 1891. The Order of the Sons of Herman is the nation's oldest fraternal benefit society. It is named after Herman the Cherusker who was captured by the Romans only to later become the leader of their army. When the Romans became oppressive, he formed an army of German tribesmen and annihilated three Roman legions in the Battle of Teutloberg Forest in 9 A.D. He is one of the greatest German folk heroes of all time. The Texas branch became autonomous in 1921. The brotherhood still exists and holds a variety of fundraising events for its various charitable interests. The lodge (which hosts the last downtown bowling alley) is located on St. Mary's, just north of Durango.

Beethoven Hall before its facade was removed during the widening of Alamo Street.

Two events in the early part of the 20th century provided an end to German culture in San Antonio. The first was World War I and the anti-German hysteria that accompanied it. German language ceased to be taught in public schools. German publications ceased. For a short time, King William Street was renamed Pershing Avenue.

The second and final nail in the coffin was prohibition. This caused the end of many German associations, which further eroded the German community. The King William neighborhood lost its appeal as prominent families moved north. Old German families disappeared into the general masses.

There are many remnants of a strong German community in San Antonio today. St Joseph's Catholic Church remains, despite being totally surrounded by a department store. For many years, it was nicknamed St. Joske's because of the surrounding Joske's store. The stained glass windows inside the church are inscribed in German. Two murals "The Assumption" and "The Annunciation," painted by Father Henry Pefferkorn, the parish's first priest, still adorn either side of the altar. The balcony still boasts one of the city's most exquisite pipe organs. Most of the parish has disappeared, but the church's cemetery still exists on the city's east side, among the city's cemetery complex. Buried here are some of San Antonio's most prominent citizens.

The German-English School also still exists, despite having classes halted in 1897 (a victim to an improved public school system which German intellectuals pushed for). The facility was purchased by George Brackenridge in 1903 and presented to the city. The building was used as Hemisfair headquarters in 1968. It is now used as a conference center for the Plaza San Antonio Hotel and still sits on South Alamo Street between the hotel's tennis courts and the Fairmount Hotel.

The original Casino Hall was torn down in 1961. The building sat at the site of Waterboard Park on Market Street. The water board, which built its headquarters so close to the hall that it was said that executives were able to enjoy a drink at the bar and keep an eye on employees next door, purchased the building in 1923. A newer Casino Club was built at the corner of Crockett and S. Presa in 1927, but the organization was quite different. The club was now a consolidation of the San Antonio Club (a literary society), and not a mainstay of German culture. The new multistoried building eventually sold to oilman Thomas Gilcrease and became known as the Gilcrease Building. The structure is now known as the Casino Building and is one of the more popular downtown apartment buildings.

The King William neighborhood has been revitalized and is now known as the King William Historic District, with many of the homes being restored to their early prominence. Most of the homes in the area are now private residences, but the Steves home at 509 King William Street has been restored to its period elegance and is open to tours. For information on a walking tour of the neighborhood, contact the San Antonio Conservation Society's office at 107 King William Street.

Read More About It:

Lich, Glen E. *The German Texans.* San Antonio: The University of Texas Institute of Texan Cultures, 1981.

The Polish in South Texas

The first group of Polish settlers came to Texas December 3, 1854. There had been other Poles who had come to Texas, but they had come primarily on their own. In 1854 a group of settlers from Upper Silesia arrived in Galveston en route to San Antonio. Upper Silesia is now in the southeastern part of Poland, but in the 1850s Upper Silesia was in the southwestern part of Prussia, separated from Poland for five centuries. Despite the separation from their homeland, the Silesians retained their Polish culture, language, and heritage.

The Poles who came to Texas were not the stereotypical poor European peasant class. The Upper Silesians were farmers, landowners, and taxpayers. They came to Texas for a variety of reasons. Primarily, they wanted a chance to own more land and to become equals rather than second-class citizens, as they were in Prussia. The Polish majority of their region was ruled by a German minority. Secondly, their region was hit by several problems that caused economic hardship. The Crimean War had forced prices to go up. In addition, the region had been hit by flood and an outbreak of cholera and typhus. Many Poles also left the region to avoid the draft into the Prussian army.

Polish immigration can also be attributed to the Reverend Leopold Moczygemba. Moczygemba was born in the Upper Silesian village of Pluzinica in 1843. At the age of 19, he left for northern Italy to join the Franciscan Order. Moczygemba wanted to serve as a missionary, and in 1852 he set sail for a remote area of the world known as Texas. The priest was first sent to New Braunfels, where he was pastor at St. Peter and Paul Church. Early church records can still be read in the handwriting of Father Moczygemba. In 1854 the young priest was sent to Castroville where he began to write to his family and friends in his homeland. Moczygemba realized the advantages the German immigrants had in this new land, and he believed his countrymen might also benefit from living in Texas.

His letters home were an overpowering catalyst for immigration. Most Poles left the region by train and then sailed by steerage class to either Galveston or to Indianola. Moczygemba suggested traveling to Indianola because it was only two weeks away from San Antonio by oxcart. The total trip took about two months.

The first settlers arrived in San Antonio on December 21, 1854. Moczygemba met them in the Alamo City and took them to an area he had chosen for them to start their own settlement. The land was in newly formed Karnes County, where the San Antonio River and Cibilo Creek met. The settlement was named Panna Maria (Polish for Virgin Mary) and is the oldest Polish settlement in the United States. The Polish settlers who came to San Antonio in the early years eventually went either to Panna Maria, Bandera (where they welcomed Slavic settlers to help populate their town), or they stayed in San Antonio. In 1855 a new settlement called Martinez was formed. The town later changed its name to St. Hedwig. The original settlers were joined by more Polish families who moved out of San Antonio in the 1870s.

The first Polish church began construction in 1855 in Panna Maria on land acquired by Moczygemba. It was finished in 1856 but destroyed by lightning in 1870. The rebuilt Church of the Immaculate Conception of the Blessed Virgin still stands today and is the oldest Polish parish in the U.S. The Bandera Polish community first built a log church and later built a sturdier St. Stanislaus in 1870. Bandera is home to the second oldest Polish parish in the U.S. St. Hedwig began its church in 1856, and San Antonio built St. Michael's in 1866.

In 1856 and 1857 one of the greatest droughts to hit Texas brought immense hardship to the Poles. The settlers became hostile towards Moczygemba for bringing them to Texas. He was also caught between his responsibilities to his people and to his new duties as the superior Franciscan in the area. Despite his repeated letters to Rome, it took many years for another Polish priest to arrive. The father left Panna Maria in 1856; a number of sources say his life may have been in danger from the angry colonists. The anger of the Poles lasted years; in 1870, missionaries wrote Rome that the "Silesians cannot forgive him up to this day" for bringing them to Texas.

In 1858 Moczygemba moved from Texas and only returned a few times to visit family. He spent most of his later life working with Polish, German, and Italian immigrants in the North. He was co-founder of the Polish seminary in Detroit and the Polish Roman Catholic Union. Moczygemba died in 1891 in Detroit and was buried in that city.

In the later 19th century, Polish settlements sprang up throughout Texas. The town of Panna Maria began to stagnate economically when the San Antonio and Aransas Pass Railroad skipped the city and decided to stop in Falls City instead. By 1902 Falls City had its own Polish church and school.

Polish life in San Antonio centered around St. Michael's Parish. The parish blossomed under the leadership of Father Thomas Moczygemba, the nephew of Father Leopold, who in 1891 became the first Polish Texan to be ordained. Under his guidance, the church was rebuilt in 1922 and opened a high school in 1935. The father died in 1941, and the church was denationalized in 1947.

The Polish influence in Texas is still felt, but not as strongly as it once was. The Polish church in San Antonio, St. Michael's, was torn down during the construction of Hemisfair Plaza. A new St. Michael's was built, but the parish was no longer predominantly Polish. In 1954 Panna Maria celebrated the centennial of their founding. In 1966 the town celebrated the millennium of Polish Christianity. The event included the dedication of a mosaic of the Virgin of Czestochowa, which President Lyndon B. Johnson gave to the community in honor of being the oldest Polish settlement in the U.S.

Also in 1966 a large grotto was built in southeastern San Antonio to commemorate the millennium. To find this somewhat obscure shrine, take the Roland exit off I-10 (the Roland exit is east of downtown), travel south to Rigsby, turn right, then turn left at Beethoven. The shrine is at 138 Beethoven.

The most fitting memorial toward Polish Texans is the reburial of Father Moczygemba in Panna Maria. When a pastor from the town traveled to Detroit on a pilgrimage to the grave of Moczygemba, he was appalled to find that not one Polish clergyman or laymen was able to take him to the gravesite. The people of Panna Maria felt the father of Polish Texans should have a more fitting memorial. With the help of Polish Americana from all over the state and with permission from all identifiable next of kin and approval from all religious and civic authorities, the remains were brought to Texas. On October 13, 1974, the body of Father Leopold Moczygemba was reinterred under the live oak tree where he had held the first mass for the colonists. Several thousand visitors attended, including two priests from Upper Silesia.

In 1986 the town was once again honored during the visit to San Antonio by Pope John Paul II, the first Polish pope. Originally, the pontiff was to visit the town, but his schedule did not permit him the pleasure. He did, however, meet with the people from Panna Maria at the grounds of Assumption Seminary. The pontiff addressed the community in his native tongue stating that "Panna Maria is well-known in Poland. Everyone knows that to here came the first Polish immigrants in the last century. Everyone remembers Father Moczygemba, who was the spiritual leader of this group and the pastor of its church."

For those wishing to sample Polish heritage, the city still supports several active Polish groups and Polish masses are still heard in San Antonio at Our Lady of Sorrows Church at the corner of St. Mary's and Mistletoe.

Read More About It:

Baker, T. Lindsay. *The Polish Texans*. San Antonio: The University of Texas Institute of Texan Cultures, 1982.

McGuire James P. and others. *The Polish Texans*. San Antonio: The University of Texas Institute of Texan Cultures, 1972.

Irish Flats

San Antonio is a city known for its Hispanic and German heritage. At one time though, the city had a thriving Irish neighborhood known as Irish Flats.

The neighborhood was originally settled by some eight to ten families that moved here from San Patricio. San Patricio (which of course is Spanish for St. Patrick) was originally settled by the Irish in the 1820s; unfortunately, they had quite a few problems with Indians, and they relocated in San Antonio. Others came to San Antonio as teamsters and settlers for the army. The area where they resettled was dubbed Irish Flats. Avenue C (now known as Broadway) was the western boundary, Sixth Street was the northern edge, Bowie was the eastern boundary, and Commerce Street marked off the southern edge. In the late 1800s, this was thought to be a remote area of San Antonio. The southwest corner of the Irish Flats area was marked by the John Stevens Homestead. Mr. Stevens was regarded as one of the leading figures of the Irish community. His home was razed in 1920 to make way for a new post office, which sat at the same site as the current post office on Alamo Plaza.

The homes in Irish Flats were unique. They combined Spanish, German, and Irish influences. A few still stand, but most were razed to accommodate a growing downtown. The neighborhood was famous for its parties, wakes, and brawls. It was regarded as one of the liveliest sections of San Antonio with many parties lasting until dawn. The Irish of San Antonio worshiped at St. Mary's Catholic Church, the city's first Catholic church to accommodate English-speaking Catholics.

After a generation, many families began to move away from the neighborhood, and it slowly faded away until it became a mere memory. A new Irish neighborhood sprang up near Ft. Sam Houston, and the community centered itself around St. Patrick's Catholic Church. Many others assimilated themselves into the suburbs and retained only their Irish surnames.

Read More About It:
Flannery, John Brendan. *The Irish Texas.* San Antonio: The University of Texas Institute of Texas Cultures, 1980.

San Antonio's Italian Neighborhood

Along with the city's other ethnic neighborhoods, San Antonio once sported an active Italian neighborhood. Most of the area that was once situated on the northwest side of downtown is now gone, removed by highway construction and urban renewal. Virtually all that remains is San Francesco de Paola Catholic Church, the Christopher Columbus Society Hall, and Columbus Park. At one time, these were the focal points of Italian life in San Antonio.

Italian immigrants first started to come to Texas in the 1870s, settling mainly in Galveston, Houston, San Antonio, Victoria County, and Thurber County. As with other immigrant groups, word of mouth from a trusted friend was the first impetus for immigration. Antonio Bruni, an Italian grocer and businessman who found success in San Antonio, convinced many Italians to come to Texas. Later, as more families made the move, advertisements from railroads and steamships that were circulated throughout Europe helped spur immigration. Most immigrants were miners, farmers, and unskilled laborers who came to work on the railroad and the mines in Victoria and Thurber counties. After the work was finished, many moved on to the urban centers.

Similar to other immigrants, the Italians clustered together in San Antonio and assisted each other as they adapted to the New World. In 1880, with the help of Antonio Bruni, the Societa Italiana De Mutuo Soccorso was formed in San Antonio, the first Italian mutual aid society in Texas. In 1890 the Christopher Columbus Society of San Antonio was formed. A combination of a fraternal association and a benevolent society, it loaned money to various families in need, taught English, and provided social activities. From its beginning, Italian was the official language of the organization. The society provided land for an Italian community church, and in 1927 San Francesca de Paola was built.

Unlike other immigrant groups, the neighborhood church did not play an overwhelming role in the Italian community. Although the community was deeply religious and had great respect for the Catholic church, many did not identify with the Irish Catholics who ran the Texas Catholic churches until the 1950s. Sicilians were traditionally anti-clerical because of the role the Roman Catholic church had in disputes between landowners and farm laborers. It was not until 1927 that San Antonio had an Italian church.

The city was also home to two Italian language news-papers: *Il Messaggiero Italiano*, which operated from 1906 to 1914 and *La Voce Patria*, which operated briefly during 1925.

As with other groups, the Italian community assimilated into American life. Families fled to the suburbs, and the neighborhood was carved up. The Christopher Columbus Society has always remained strong (though English became the official language in 1946), and the group now accepts some non-Italians. Today, it holds famous Italian dinners and donates to many worthwhile projects. The statue of Columbus in the adjacent park was donated in 1957. For over 100 years, the organization has been a cornerstone of the Italian community in San Antonio.

Read More About It:

Belfiglio, Cavaliere Valentine. *Italian Experience in Texas.* Austin: Eakin Press, 1983.

The Italian Texans (pamphlet). San Antonio: The University of Texas Institute of Texan Culture, 1973.

The Chinese in San Antonio

San Antonio never did have a Chinatown, so to speak; however, the city does have a rich history involving Chinese settlers.

The Chinese Exclusion Act was passed in 1882 to hold back the number of Chinese immigrating to the U.S. By that time, there were quite a few Chinese already living on this side of the Pacific, mainly working on the railroads. By 1890 about 50 families settled here after the completion of the Southern Pacific Railroad.

Many Chinese were still immigrating from Asia and were settling in Mexico, hoping that some day America would change its mind and allow them to become U.S. citizens.

The Chinese in Mexico got a chance to show their allegiance to their neighbors to the north when General Pershing pursued Pancho Villa. The general was quite surprised when a community of Spanish-speaking Chinese supplied his troops with food, staples, and other supplies during his campaign in Mexico. When Pershing was ready to return to Ft. Sam Houston, Villa swore that he would hang every "Chino" who assisted the general. Pershing lead his aides to safety back in San Antonio and convinced Congress to give them special consideration and grant them citizenship. The Chinese were so grateful that many named their children after the general. Names such as Black Jack Wong and Pershing Yium are just a few of the variations found. When General Pershing died, the greatest outpouring of sympathy at his funeral at Arlington National Cemetery was from San Antonio's Chinese community.

When World War I broke out, many of the Chinese were employed at Ft. Sam Houston. After the war they began to rely less on government employment and set up their own community structure. Cafes, laundries, and grocery stores were the most common businesses set up. As soon as a businessman got on his feet, he would send for the rest of his family. Interestingly, the Chinese community blended quickly into the cosmopolitan city of San Antonio. Unlike other cities, discrimination was virtually nonexistent. Many Chinese learned to speak Spanish before English, a curiosity for out-of-town visitors.

A Chinese language school existed on 215 San Saba Street—the first in Texas. In the early years, classes were taught from 4:30 P.M. to 7:30 P.M. six days a week—this was in addition to public school attendance. A Chinese mission was set up in what was originally the Spanish Governor's Palace. The mission became the Chinese Baptist Church in 1923, the first such church in the South. The church's original offices were located at 509 ½ Commerce Street. They later moved to a new building on Avenue B. Fraternal organizations were also formed including Chinese Free Masons and a Chinese Optimist Club.

The Chinese quickly became assimilated into San Antonio life, contributing in many ways. Theodore Wu, a teacher at the school, was one of the founders of Boysville. The Chinese Baptist Church still exists on Avenue B. The Chinese school closed in 1947, but the Chinese Community Council reopened it in 1971 on the city's north side, opening classes to the public.

Katherine Stinson and the
Stinson Flying School

The early days of aviation were a most exciting time. Young daredevils filled the skies, and thousands gathered to watch. The few who dared to enter a flying machine were among the era's most popular celebrities. Most of the pilots in the early days were men. Few believed that the skies were a place for women. Katherine Stinson thought differently.

As a young woman, Katherine was looking for a way to raise money for a trip to Europe. She had heard that pilots could earn $1,000 a day, an unheard-of amount in 1910. After receiving the skeptical approval of her parents, the nineteen-year-old set out to learn to fly. It took two years before she had the opportunity to soar through the skies. Finding a flight instructor was a feat in itself because there were only 200 licensed pilots in the world in 1912, and only three were women.

Stinson sought the help of Max Lillie of Chicago. Lillie was not overenthusiastic about taking on a female student, who was barely five feet tall and just over 100 pounds. Stinson proved to the famous aviator that she possessed many qualities, other than sex and strength, that would assist her as a pilot. After a mere four hours of lessons, she soloed. She acquired her license on July 12, 1912, from the Federation Aeronautique Internationale, becoming the fourth woman pilot in America.

Soon after, onlookers flocked to fairs and open fields to see the "flying schoolgirl." The small-framed woman with long curly brown hair was a definite sight to see. Stinson was one of a proud few who introduced flying to the general public by her appearances in air shows. In 1913 Katherine Stinson opened the Stinson Aviation Company in Hot Springs, Arkansas, along with her mother. The Stinson family built, sold, and rented aircraft at the Hot Springs facility. The venture was a true family business, as they were joined by her younger siblings, Marjorie, Jack, and Eddie.

In 1913 the family was convinced by Max Lillie to move to San Antonio. Lillie found the mild winters and the terrain perfect for year-round flying. He had convinced the Army to let him use the Fort Sam Houston parade ground as a landing strip. The Army was determined to discover if flying could have military applications. The sight of Katherine Stinson flying over the city, performing stunts including loop to loops, became a familiar sight. Stinson taught herself the difficult and dangerous stunt and was the first woman to perform it. It soon became part of her flying repertoire.

Katherine was more than an excellent pilot, she was also a first-rate mechanic. In the early days, she traveled from show to show by train, reassembling her plane at each stop. She often was teased by the other pilots when it came to her meticulous habits regarding her aircraft.

Her reputation as a pilot grew as she continued to tour. In Los Angeles she spelled out the word CAL with fireworks, becoming the first pilot to skywrite at night. In London she amazed the English by flying around the House of Parliament and St. Paul's Cathedral. She toured Canada at a time when most people of that nation had never seen a flying machine. In 1916 she traveled to Japan and China, where she was overwhelmed by the adoration of her fans. Twenty-five thousand fans turned out in Tokyo to watch her fly. Fan clubs sprang up all over Japan. She made thirty-two appearances in China, including a private show for Chinese leaders. Her fame had spread worldwide.

When World War I broke out, the U.S. Army, recognizing the significance of air power, asked for pilots to volunteer for service. Katherine Stinson offered her talents to the Army but was turned down because she was a woman. The aviatrix had to be satisfied with raising money for the Red Cross as her contribution to the war effort.

Since military flying was out, Stinson decided to concentrate her efforts on other flying accomplishments. On

December 17, 1917, Katherine left San Diego for an attempt to break a world record in distance flying. Leaving at 7:31 A.M., in a special plane designed to fly at the breakneck speed of 85 miles per hour and hold enough fuel to be able to travel 700 miles, she set out for San Francisco. At 4:41 P.M. she landed in San Francis with two gallons of fuel left. Her trip of 610 miles set a new world record. She had covered more miles and had been airborne longer than any man or woman pilot ever. With her place in aviation history secure, she again applied to the Army for a position as a reconnaissance pilot but was again turned down.

In 1918 she began flying air mail and set another distance record on a mail run from Chicago to New York. Because of unfavorable winds, she landed 150 miles short of the city and had to make an emergency landing in Binghamton, New York; but, her distance of 783 miles was enough to break her own record. Flying mail paled in comparison to flying for the Army. She finally gained her acceptance into the military by volunteering as an ambulance driver. Stinson served in London and France during the war and paid dearly for her efforts.

As the war drew to a close, she contracted tuberculosis. The treatment was a warm climate and rest. Her flying days were over. She retired to a more passive life in New Mexico. Katherine Stinson married former World War I airman Miguel Otero, Jr., in 1928 and lived until 1977, when she died at age eighty-six in Santa Fe.

Katherine Stinson's younger sister Marjorie and her brother Eddie also made their mark on aviation history. At the age of 18, Marjorie earned her pilot's license and soon became known around the air show circuit. In 1915 she began training pilots at the Stinson Flying School located at the site of city-owned airport Stinson Field. She was the first woman to own and operate a flying school in the United States. Many of her students were Canadians eager to join the allied war effort in World War I. One of her students was John Frost, son of the founder of Frost National Bank.

Though she and her sister could not fly for the U.S. Army, they could train pilots. Marjorie trained over eighty pilots who later served in the war.

Like her sister, Marjorie flew air mail. She delivered the first air mail in Texas covering the expansive San Antonio to Seguin route. She also worked for the U.S. War Department for fifteen years as an aeronautical draftsman. Marjorie Stinson died in 1975.

The only Stinson to fly for the Army was Eddie Stinson. Before World War I, Eddie and Marjorie ran a flying school using the parade ground at Fort Sam Houston as a landing strip. Eddie Stinson was the only family member to lose his life in a plane accident. He died on January 25, 1932, during an emergency landing in Chicago, when an engine on the plane he was flying quit working.

Read More About It:
Roger, Mary Beth, Smith, Sherry A., and Scott, Janelle D. *We Can Fly: Stories of Katherine Stinson & Other Gutsy Texas Women.* Published by Ellen C. Temple in cooperation with the Texas Foundation for Women's Resources, Austin: 1983.

Eugene O. Goldbeck

San Antonio's most industrious and famous photographer, Eugene Goldbeck, traveled the world for over eighty years. He revolutionized panoramic photography to such an extent that his work is recognized throughout the world. Born in San Antonio in 1891 (or 1892 as his alternate birth certificate indicates), Goldbeck was bitten by the photo bug at an early age. By age nine he had already included in his early portfolio a shot of President McKinley—an extraordinary feat if you remember that photography was still in its infancy. By age 15 he was selling photos of his classmates at school and soon began supplying photographs to both the *San Antonio Light* and the *Express*, making him the first person to do so.

In 1910 the young photographer graduated from Main Avenue High School and began working as a full-time photographer. His skill with the camera was recognized throughout town, even by the military. When Lt. Benjamin Foulois made the military's first flight on the parade ground at Fort Sam Houston, Goldbeck was there to record the event.

Two years later he purchased his first Cirkut panoramic camera. He immediately began experimenting with this new technology. One of his earliest shots is of the U.S. Army's entire air force in flight, a total of three planes. During World War I, Goldbeck joined the Photo Division of the U.S. Signal Corps and made ties with the military that would last a lifetime.

After the war Goldbeck returned to San Antonio. For a short time he worked with Fox Photo. He later formed the National Photo and News Service, based out of a two-story building in his backyard on the south side. The city was only a base of operations, because Goldbeck was a traveler.

During his lifetime, he shot photos in Japan, the Soviet Union, Egypt, and the South Pacific, just to name a few.

The photographer lived into his nineties. He set such a high standard for panoramic photography that his work is instantly recognized. In his final years he sold autographed photos from his home on the south side for twenty-five dollars. Today, a signed Goldbeck is worth five times that.

Read More About Him:

Burleson, Clyde W. and Hickman, E. Jessica. *The Panoramic Photography of Eugene O. Goldbeck.* Austin: University of Texas Press, 1986.

The Lucchese Family

For over 100 years, the term Lucchese meant only one thing, the finest quality boots. The company that has come to be associated with first-class footwear was founded by Salvatore "Sam" Lucchese, a native of Palermo, Italy, who was born in 1866 into a bootmaking family. In 1882 he arrived in Galveston and set up shop in San Antonio a year later at the age of 17. Shoemaking was a popular business for Italian immigrants because it took so little financial outlay to begin a business.

Because of a large supply of army personnel at Fort Sam, The Lucchese Boot Company always had a supply of customers. The shop on 317 E. Houston made riding boots for graduating cadets in the Army Air Corps until they were discontinued as part of the uniform in 1934. The Army followed suit in 1938. Lucchese's boots continue to be popular with the cadet corps at Texas A&M.

But the Luccheses did just fine without the military, because everybody seemed to want a pair of custom-made boots. After World War II, second-generation bootmaker Cosimo Lucchese would often raise the price of their product to cut back on the demand and insure they would not have to rush. When the demand fell, Cosimo would lower the price again. Many prominent Texas families and famous Americans have had the Luccheses make their boots. Grandson Sam Lucchese has made boots for Lyndon Johnson. In 1898 the founder crafted a pair for Teddy Roosevelt when he was in town with the Rough Riders. General "Hap" Arnold, head of the U.S. Army Air Corp in World War II, wore Luccheses, as did Generals Eisenhower, MacArthur, and Patton. Gene Autry, Bob Hope, John Wayne, Jimmy Dean, Gregory Peck, Jimmy Stewart, and Bing Crosby also were measured for a pair of custom-made boots.

The boot company stayed in the family for many years, passing from Salvatore Lucchese to son Cosimo Lucchese to grandson Sam Lucchese.

Salvatore Lucchese's daughter Josephine also made a name for herself outside the family business. With her debut as a coloratura soprano in New York in 1922, she became the first American-studied soprano to be considered a serious opera talent. Madame Lucchese became known as "The American Nightingale" as her talents took her to Milan, New York, and other sites around the world. She sang opposite some of the leading tenors of her time, including Tito Schipa and Giovanni Martinelli. For many years she was the leading soprano of the Philadelphia Grand Opera Company. From 1957 until 1970 she was on the music faculty at the University of Texas and continued to give private voice lessons to exceptional students.

In 1984 the Acme Boot Company purchased the Lucchese Boot Company. Though the boots are no longer handmade, they still represent the top of the line when it comes to quality footwear.

Gutzon Borglum and the Mill Race Studio

One of the most intriguing artists to pass through San Antonio was noted sculptor Gutzon Borglum. Borglum came to the city in 1925 to create a memorial for the Trail Drivers Museum. He immediately won the respect of the people of Texas, who treated him as the ultimate celebrity when he toured the state with a model of his creation. Borglum stayed in the city for many years, working out of a studio in Brackenridge Park. The studio, a former water works facility, was modified by the artist and was the site of some of his most famous creations. It was here that Borglum created his famous statue of Woodrow Wilson for the Polish government.

Borglum was a man of many contradictions. He was an avowed antisemite, who often spoke about the "Jewish Problem." Often he preached against the so-called Jewish Establishment and their control of the banking industry. However, many of his patrons, financial backers, and close friends were Jewish. Supreme Court Justice Felix Frankfurter, like many of his contemporaries, accepted the self-proclaimed antisemite as a valued friend who was uncompromising in his beliefs. When Hitler began carrying out a plan to exterminate Jewish citizens, Borglum, the man of many contradictions, became an outspoken opponent of the fuhrer. When Hitler invaded Poland, one of his first acts was to destroy Borglum's statue of Woodrow Wilson.

The artist took an active role in the politics of the day. He allowed Czechoslovakian rebels to train on his Connecticut estate during World War I. He investigated the aircraft industry for corruption during the first World War. He was an advisor to presidents and chiefs of state. He became a powerful member of the Ku Klux Klan in a time when the racist organization was trying to mainstream their cause.

When Borglum arrived in San Antonio, he had just been fired by a commission to create a monument in Stone Mountain, Georgia, honoring Confederate heroes. He left Georgia a fugitive for destroying a vital model of the uncompleted sculpture. When in San Antonio, he quickly set up shop at Brackenridge Park in his Mill Race Studio. After the creation of the Trail Drivers monument, he left for South Dakota, where he was commissioned to create his most famous work, a giant carving of four ex-presidents on Mount Rushmore.

Borglum left a large legacy. His art is displayed in the White House, the New York Metropolitan Museum of Art, in Los Angeles, Detroit, Newark, Chicago, and San Antonio. He designed the flame in the Statue of Liberty's torch. He was the head of the Texas Beautification Plan and proposed ideas, such as a Corpus Christi waterfront, that were years ahead of their time. As for San Antonio, his contributions to the city are mostly forgotten. Throughout the carving of Mount Rushmore, he wintered in San Antonio while working on his other commissions. He left for California in the 1930s after losing out on the Alamo Cenotaph commission.

His studio was turned over to the San Antonio Art League, who used it for young artists for many years. Some of his greatest pieces were created there. After many years, the building was abandoned. It sat in quiet ruins for many years, adjacent to the Brackenridge Golf Course parking lot. Today the structure has been refurbished and is now the offices for local architects.

Read More About Him:
Scaff, Howard and Audrey Karl. *Six Wars at a Time, the Life and Times of Gutzon Borglum.* Sioux Falls, South Dakota: Augustana College, 1985.

Father Carmelo Tranchese

To the people of the west side, Father Carmelo Tranchese is one of the most respected figures to ever touch their lives. Tranchese became pastor of Our Lady of Guadalupe in July of 1932. At the time, the church served 12,000 desperately poor parishioners. The church was deeply in debt, the building was in poor shape, and the parish house had only apple crates for chairs. The neighborhood was in even worse shape. The west side was one of the worst slums in the U.S.; its poverty reached a level the priest thought unimaginable in America. The death rate was three times the national average.

A bad situation got worse the next year when the National Industrial Recovery Act established a minimum wage of 25 cents an hour. Most of the westside workers were pecan shellers who worked for the ridiculously low wage of $1.50 a week. Instead of receiving a raise, the pecan shellers were dismissed from their jobs and replaced with machines, causing an already bad situation to worsen. The father, who was already 51 years old, worked with then San Antonio mayor C. K. Quin to collect food for over 7000 desperate, out-of-work westsiders.

The priest was also appalled by the lack of decent housing for the people of his parish. Most of the westside residents lived in small shacks without adequate plumbing. Father Tranchese convinced the Junior Chamber of Commerce to purchase the slums, tear them down, and rebuild adequate housing. Unfortunately, the shacks were torn down, but nothing was built to replace them.

Tranchese worked with U.S. Congressman Maury Maverick to convince the federal government to build affordable housing for the people of his parish. Despite numerous setbacks, including a Supreme Court ruling challenging the constitutionality of public housing and numerous threats on the father's life, the priest was able to convince the National Housing Authority to build the Apache-Alazon Courts in 1939, the first public housing project in the nation. The project had to be scaled down because the landowners charged an exorbitant price for the property. Still, the new apartments were a vast improvement for those lucky enough to get in. Rents ranged from $8.75 to $11.25 depending on the apartment's size, which easily compared with the rents charged to those living in the shanties.

Tranchese also worked to establish a child health clinic, a nursery school, and a playground and helped form a class where young girls could learn their native dances. The father retired in 1953 in Louisiana where he died three years later. The priest was a recognized scholar and held a high position at the University of Naples where he taught physics and literature before coming to America. He spoke five languages: French, Spanish, Italian, English, and Latin. He also taught at Denver's Sacred Heart College. To the people of the west side, he is remembered as Father Carmelo, one of the first people who worked to improve the quality of their lives.

Dr. Aureliano Urrutia

Thousands of people each day drive by a small private park on Hildebrand near Broadway, next to the Southwestern Bell building. Many know that this is Pioneer Park, a private picnic ground for employees of the phone company. It's named for Bell Telephone Pioneers, a group of employees with 18 years of service to the company. Many have also noticed the ornate gates with the name Urrutia across the top. Who was Urrutia and why all the sculptures?

The park was originally the summer home of Dr. Aureliano Urrutia, a famed surgeon who liked the area near the San Antonio River's headwaters because they reminded him of his native Mexico. Urrutia gained his first notoriety at the turn of the century, when he was the personal physician of President Porfirio Diaz. In 1913 the doctor was appointed Minister of the Interior during the dictatorship of Victoriano Huerta. It was rumored that Urrutia was a henchman for Huerta, and it was also said that he cut out the tongue of an opposition leader. It was also the doctor who sent an ultimatum to Woodrow Wilson demanding that he recognize the Mexican government as legitimate. Wilson sent the marines.

Urrutia went into exile because of the Mexican Revolution and eventually settled in San Antonio. Soon after moving to San Antonio, he gained world-wide recognition when he separated a pair of Siamese twins in 1917. Although only one twin lived, he was often introduced as the doctor who separated the infants. Urrutia built a beautiful mansion on Broadway and dubbed it Quinta Urrutia. This castle-like home, with its beautiful gardens, sculptures, and fountains, was a showplace and gathering spot for the social elite in the 1920s. The doctor opened a clinic downtown and built a summer home dubbed Miraflores on the northern edge of town.

Another fantastic story about the doctor allegedly occurred while he was attending a party at the St. Anthony Hotel. It is said that General Frederick Funston was also attending the event. Funston and Urrutia had a few confrontations during the tumultuous days of the Mexican Revolution, and there was no love lost between the two. According to the legend, Urrutia flashed the general "the evil eye," and Funston fell over and died. (Funston did indeed die at the St. Anthony Hotel during a social event on February 19, 1917. As the band began to play "Blue Danube," Funston collapsed and died of heart failure.)

Despite the persistent rumors, Urrutia was a great doctor. He performed 6,000 operations before retiring at age 88 in 1959. He fathered 18 children, many of whom became doctors and served with their father. In 1962 he sold Miraflores to USAA Insurance for $300,000. (USAA later sold the park and its headquarters to Southwestern Bell.) Quinta Urrutia was sold a short time later and eventually became home to a car dealership located at 3225 Broadway.

Urrutia, who was famous for always wearing an opera cape, died in 1975 at the age of 104.

Dionico Rodriguez

Thousands of San Antonians have caught the bus on Broadway near the Alamo Heights H.E.B. grocery store and have sat in a peculiar bus stop that appears to be made of petrified wood. But few know the story behind the unique piece of artwork, and the man who made it. The city's most accessible work of art was built at the corner of Broadway and Patterson in 1931, by Dionico Rodriguez. The bus shelter was donated to the city of Alamo Heights by the Alamo Cement company and has only been moved once, a few feet when the street was paved.

Many are fooled when looking at the bus stop, believing that the shelter is made of petrified wood. Actually it's made of cement, Rodriguez's chosen medium. The artist, who was born in Mexico City in 1891, learned the unusual art form from a Spanish national who showed him a unique chemical process to make cement look like petrified wood. One of Rodriguez's earliest patrons was Dr. Aureliano Urrutia who introduced him to Charles Baumberger, Sr., founder of Alamo Cement.

Baumberger commissioned several pieces, including the Alamo Heights shelter, a fish pond at the cement plant, and a unique fence also at the Alamo Cement plant headquarters. (Now that Alamo Cement has moved, the fate of these two pieces is in question.) Two examples of his work can also be found in Brackenridge Park. A bridge near the park's headquarters and an old entrance to the Sunken Gardens were both his creations. The gate to Sunken Gardens reads "Chinese Tea Gardens" rather than Japanese Sunken Gardens. That's because the entryway was made during World War II when anti-Japanese sentiment was high, and the name of the gardens was changed. Other examples of his work can be found at private residences throughout the city, as well as in Memphis, Little Rock, New York City, Chattanooga, Cuba, and Mexico.

Rodriguez was very secretive about the chemical process that transformed the appearance of the cement. Once he started, he used simple tools such as a fork, knife, and spoon to shape his creations. Rodriguez also preferred to use local cement in his work because it contained no sand or mortar.

Rodriguez died in San Antonio in 1955, leaving behind numerous pieces of art made from his mysterious process.

The Alamo Heights bus/trolley stop in 1929.

O. P. Schnabel and his Antilitter Campaign

Every time you walk down a San Antonio street and notice a trash receptacle placed on the corner, you can thank O. P. Schnabel. Each time you notice an area merchant cleaning up the outside of his business where a Beautify San Antonio award is displayed, once again thank O. P. Schnabel. What began as a one-man campaign to keep litter off the street has now blossomed into a city-wide effort. A cleaner San Antonio was the end result of a forty-year effort of a man known simply as Mr. Clean.

Schnabel started as a manager of Jefferson Standard Life Insurance Company in 1919. A successful insurance salesman, he rewarded himself in 1947 with a trip to Switzerland. He was inspired by the cleanliness of the European cities, and he returned home with a goal to stamp out litter locally. While many people talk of making a change, Schnabel put his plan into action. He founded the Beautify San Antonio Association and started one of the first antilitter campaigns ever in America. He helped the city acquire trash receptacles for street corners. His organization offered awards to area merchants who beautified their grounds. He founded the Beautify Texas Council and often could be seen picking up trash on the streets of downtown.

Born Otto Phillip Schnabel, San Antonians jested that O. P. stood for Old Pushbroom. The city honored the antilitter pioneer by naming a park after him on the northwest side.

Schnabel's trademark was a shiny new penny glued to a business card wishing people good luck and asking them not to litter. He started giving away pennies in 1926, and he once estimated that he handed out $70,000, one penny at a time.

Pola Negri

Many celebrities traveling through San Antonio become enchanted with the Alamo City's charm. Occasionally, someone is so taken by the city that they decide to make it their home. Such was the case of silent film star Pola Negri. Ms. Negri was born Apollonia Barbara Chapulex in Lipno, Poland, where she became a star of stage and screen in Eastern Europe. She became one of the first foreign film stars to achieve success in Hollywood. She appeared in such silent classics as *Bella Donna*, *The Spanish Dancer*, *Forbidden Paradise*, *Shadows of Paris*, *Woman on Trial*, and *A Woman of the World*. Her most famous role was that of Carmen in the classic *Gypsy Blood*. Her first talking motion picture was *Woman Commands*, but her career did not progress into the era of talking pictures. She was often linked romantically with many of Hollywood's most famous leading men, including Charlie Chaplin. Her one great love was for Rudolph Valentino, who died in 1926.

She lived in Europe in the 1930s and returned to the U.S. during the second World War. In 1957 she made a visit to San Antonio with her local friend Margaret West and was taken by the city. In 1959 she moved to the city and basically retired from show business. Despite many motion picture offers, she preferred to lead a quiet life writing her memoirs and enjoying local life. She accepted one final offer in 1968, a Disney project entitled *The Moonspinners*. In 1968 she was awarded the Hemisfair Film Festival Award for her contributions.

Many believed that Ms. Negri was a recluse, a faded star who jealously guarded her privacy. Such was not the case. Though she did not capitalize on her fame, she was an active member of the community. She was on the board of directors for the San Antonio Symphony and of San Antonio Little

Theatre. She was a member of St. Anthony's Catholic Church and a supporter of the Shrine of Our Lady of Czestochowa on the city's southeast side. In 1964 she donated her 700-volume library containing many rare books to Trinity University. In 1970 she donated her rare recording collection to St. Mary's University. In 1984 she contributed to Henry Cisneros' campaign for mayor.

Negri spent her last 25 years in the Alamo City living quietly in a condo on the north side. She died August 1, 1987, of an inoperable tumor.

SECTION III

SAN ANTONIO PLACES

The Tower Life Building

For over sixty years, the Tower Life Building has been the signature of San Antonio's skyline. Built in 1929, it was the tallest building west of the Mississippi River until the 1950s. The building, located on the corner of St. Mary's and Villita streets, dominated downtown and could be seen throughout the city.

The structure was originally known as the Smith-Young Tower after its builders, the Smith Brothers and their partner, lawyer J. W. Young. The Smith Brothers purchased the land that was originally Bowen's Island in 1923. Their hope was to build a complex of buildings that would equal the impact of Rockefeller Center in New York. The centerpiece was to be the Smith-Young Tower. The Bowen Island Skyscrapers (as the project was known in its early stages) included the Plaza Hotel (now the Granada Homes), the Federal Reserve Building (now the Mexican Consulate), the A. B. Frank Company Wholesale and Drygoods Building (now the City Public Service Building), and a host of other buildings, including a Chevrolet dealership and a Montgomery Wards. Most of the buildings, including the tower, were designed by Altee B. Ayres and his son Robert M. Ayres.

The Tower has numerous features that set it apart from other skyscrapers. According to promotional literature, it offered the finest elevator service in the world. If you walk into the lobby today (which is virtually unchanged), you'll notice the original elevator doors complete with the old Smith-Young logo. The building also featured observation decks on the 7th, 22nd, 27th, and 30th floors. They have long since been closed to the public, but workers in the building still occasionally sneak out onto the 30th floor deck. At one time, for 50 cents, you could ride the elevator to the 28th floor and walk up a flight of stairs to the best view in Texas. Many of the patrons who visited the observation deck have scratched their names in the copper moldings, and their scratchings are still visible today.

The building also featured a shopping arcade in the basement that connected the Tower to the coffee shop in the Plaza Hotel across the street. This has also been closed. A discerning eye will also notice some figures that circle the upper floors of the building. These are carved gargoyles that were added to protect the building from evil spirits. The practice seems antiquated today but was quite common in its day.

The Tower Life Building was also home to the first Sears store in San Antonio. Sears opened on March 7, 1929, three months before the formal opening of the skyscraper. It took up the basement and the first four floors and featured three of its own elevators. Display cases that have been converted into windows are still visible on the street level. The Sears store was located there for ten years. The offices above the store featured the most up-to-date amenities ever offered in a San Antonio office building. These included water coolers on every floor, bathrooms with hot and cold running water, and telephone and electric outlets in every office.

The Tower officially opened on June 1, 1929, at a cost of $2,500,000. It has gone through many name changes; its first was in February, 1938, when the Smith-Young Tower was redubbed the Pan American Building. In 1942 it was bought by the San Antonio Transit Company and became the Transit Building. The building was purchased in 1943 by the Citizens Republic Life Insurance Company, and in 1962 the company changed its name to the Tower Life Insurance Company and changed the name of the building to match.

The Tower Life Building has had its share of historic moments. Dwight D. Eisenhower and the Third U.S. Army had its offices there in 1941. The building has also been used for everything from a mooring mast for a blimp to a performance site for a duo of aerialists.

Photo published in the San Antonio Light *on April 1, 1938 showing the meteor that hit the Smith-Young Tower (now the Tower Life Building).*

At the time the building was being constructed, San Antonio was experiencing an unprecedented building boom that reflected the optimism of the city in the 1920s. This explosion of new construction was halted by the Depression, and the San Antonio skyline remained virtually unchanged for the next fifty years. Other buildings constructed in this boom era include the Frost National Bank Building (1922), the Medical Arts Building (1926), the Express News Building (1929), the Majestic Theatre (1929), the Nix Medical Building (1929), and the Alamo National Bank Building (1929).

In 1928 the Milam Building on the corner of Travis Street and Soledad was built. This twenty-one-story high-rise was the first building in the world to be totally air conditioned. So new was the idea of air conditioning that advertisements had to be placed in local newspapers to convince business-men of the comfort of the new system:

> At the time I moved in, I was a little prejudiced against the air conditioning system. I don't know why, for I had never taken the time to investigate it. But after moving in, I prize it above all other features in the building. Because of the air conditioning system, I can keep my windows closed and keep out the street noise. This absence of noise . . . makes this the most restful building.
>
> Then, too, with the windows closed, I can keep the wind out. If there is anything that is irritating to me it is to have my papers . . . blown out of order. Here I can lay the lightest papers about my desk without fear.

> Earl Wilson, R. E. Wilson Co.
> *San Antonio Evening News*
> November 9, 1928

The original air conditioning system lasted more than sixty years. For many years, huge chunks of ice had to be hauled to the basement to cool the building.

The Milam Building became home to the biggest names in the oil industry. Shell, Mobil, and Humble (later Exxon) all had their headquarters there before migrating to Houston. So many deals were made in the coffee shop downstairs that it was nicknamed the "Linoleum Club." Many wildcatters set up offices in the booths of the restaurant.

The Milam Building was home to the Texas Railroad Commission (which handed out oil leases, thus attracting oil companies to the building), its own post office, beauty shop, barber shop, clothing stores, and many more amenities for the modern businessman. The lobby was beautifully decorated with Saltillo tile from Mexico, cherry wood railings for the stairs, hand-carved Corinthian columns, and a fourteen-foot ceiling.

The adjacent parking garage was torn down in 1987 to make way for the new NBC Tower. Gone with the garage is the Mobil horse that flew over the gas station there for fifty years.

Though downtown has changed much over the past twenty years, the Milam Building, with its huge Texas flag flying above it, continues to be one of the city's most prestigious addresses.

The Alamo National Bank

For over 50 years that the Alamo Bank Building towered over downtown, its famous neon sign atop the structure was a long-standing landmark for the people of San Antonio. The bank has its own special place in the city's history. It was formed on the grounds of the Alamo when several prominent businessmen met at the Hugo, Schmeltzer Wholesale Grocery Company (which was located where the Alamo barracks now are) in November of 1890. Charles Hugo was selected as the first chief executive for the Alamo National Bank of San Antonio which received its charter on Texas Independence Day of 1891.

Its first location was at the corner of Soledad and Commerce in the Kampmann Building. The bank built its own building in 1899 at the corner of Presa and Commerce. This building at 316 E. Commerce was designed by Altee B. Ayres and James Wahrenberger and was originally only five stories tall.

The merchants on Commerce Street found it necessary to expand their thoroughfare to keep up with the bustling growth of San Antonio, so in 1915 they privately funded the widening of their street. To complete the task, the Alamo Bank Building had to be moved back from Commerce Street. The building was literally picked up and moved back 15 feet without disrupting service (or as legend says, without disrupting elevator service). Three more stories were added to the building in 1916. The wrought iron gates on the front of the building still sport the letters ANB, though the Alamo National Bank has not occupied that building for over 60 years.

Crews lift and move the old Alamo Bank Building to allow the widening of Commerce Street.

In 1929 the bank had once again outgrown its facility and began to build its new home at 154 Commerce. The new office was finished in 1930 at a cost of 2.5 million dollars. Its 23 stories towered over downtown. A trip into the lobby is a must, its art deco interior and distinctive stained glass are a visual treat. Atop the building rested one of San Antonio's most famous landmarks, the multicolored neon Alamo National Bank sign. This sign could be seen for miles around and was prominently displayed in every photograph of the city skyline. In 1986 the bank was taken over by the Mercantile Texas Corporation, which renamed the bank M Bank Alamo, while the building became the Alamo Bank Building. The sign atop the building was replaced with one which bore the new name. The railing atop the building was gold plated for a nice visual touch.

According to literature from the old Alamo National Bank, the sign was more than a display of neon, it was a weather indicator. When the lights of the neon spiral rose from the bottom to the top, the temperature was rising. When the spiral lights were lit from top to bottom, the temperature was falling. A fully lit spiral meant no change in the weather. Flashing lights meant rain.

The M Bank people have a notorious record when it comes to San Antonio. The same corporation was also responsible for tearing down the Bluebonnet Hotel. The Alamo National Bank may no longer exist, but its memory is alive in every Goldbeck photo of downtown. M Bank eventually failed and has now been replaced by Bank One.

Old Theatres

Like any major city, San Antonio has had its share of old theatres. Many have come and gone, though the city has been lucky to keep a few of the gems.

Downtown Theatres

Downtown was once a vibrant place for moviegoers. If you stood on the corner of Houston and St. Mary's, you could see the State, the Alameda, the Texas, the Majestic, the Empire, and the Aztec. San Antonio is one of the few cities in Texas to have so many downtown theatres left.

The Majestic - The Majestic opened in June, 1929, as one of the premier palaces of its time. One Texas theatre owner claimed the San Antonio Majestic "will be as great an influence for good as the church." It was designed by Chicago architect John Eberson, who created elaborate theatres across America, including four in Texas. Eberson is known as the father of the "atmospheric theatre." It was Eberson who first created the idea of stars and clouds on the auditorium's ceiling. The Majestic is recognized as his most elaborate creation. Eberson once wrote, "To be a successful theatre architect, one must be a showman. I want to create theatres where pictures can be enjoyed in restful and beautiful surroundings rather than one that would be a mere flaunt of lavishness." The theatre and fourteen stories of office space were built for two million dollars and took thirteen months to complete. Its switchboard was powerful enough to supply the electricity for a town of 15,000. The Majestic was initially built to host both movies and vaudeville. It closed for a short time in 1930 and reopened as a first run movie house.

The theatre's interior is a mixture of Spanish and Moorish design and includes Eberson's trademark ceiling that is sky blue with twinkling stars and a parade of passing clouds produced by a concealed machine. The left side of the auditorium is patterned after a Spanish colonial palace and the right side after a Moorish castle. Each side is decorated with tiled towers, plazas, false balconies, a dozen doves, and one peacock. Ebersol designed the complex interior to be built with plaster. The metal and wood-looking fixtures are all actually plaster. Plaster was the building material of choice because it was the least expensive. The lobby comes complete with a series of balconies, staircases, a fountain with an unclothed beauty named "Sweet Nymph," and a large aquarium.

One of the interesting features of the theatre is the special balcony for black patrons. It was only accessible from an entrance on College Street and is barely visible from the rest of the theatre. The Majestic closed in 1974 and later was transformed into a performing arts theatre featuring touring rock bands and Broadway shows. In 1988 the city acquired the Majestic and the adjacent Empire and leased them for a dollar a year to La Casa, a nonprofit group. The group raised almost five million dollars to restore the theatre.

San Antonio architect Milton Babbitt, along with movie palace restorers Ray Shephardson and Sonya White, worked to painstakingly refurbish the theatre to its former elegance. Local craftsman, some of whom had fathers and grandfathers who worked on the theatre, were hired for the restoration. Samples of the old carpet and seat covers were found and reloomed. Extensive work was done in the basement to provide additional dressing rooms and storage space to alleviate the use of the cramped backstage. Space was leased in the adjacent garage to build a new bar so the lobby could be restored to its original size. The Majestic is now home to the San Antonio Symphony and is the centerpiece of a new performing arts district and the redeveloped Houston Street. The upper floors are being converted into apartments.

The Majestic Theatre during the premier of Audie Murphy's To Hell and Back.

Earl Abel at the Texas Theatre organ.

The Aztec - This large theatre at the corner of Commerce and St. Mary's was built in 1926 as a lavish atmosphere theatre. The builders sent a team of designers to Mexico to study the ancient Mayan, Aztec, and Toltec ruins. The team's drawings were used in designing replicas used in the interior of the theatre. The Hall of Columns at Mitla was the inspiration for the foyer. Each column is topped by a mask representing the Aztec moon goddess. The chandelier in the lobby is a replica of an Aztec sacrificial stone and was painted with bloodstains in the grooves to give it that authentic touch. The original fire curtain depicted the meeting of Cortez and Montezuma. The arch separating the curtain and the orchestra pit is decorated with the symbol of Quetzacoatl, chief god of the Aztecs. The Mayan theme is quite impressive, but it lost some of the impact when it was divided into a three-screen theatre in 1964.

Developer Hap Veltman wanted to make the theatre into a performing arts center (possibly a home for the symphony) and use the Karotkin Building for condos. The death of Veltman in the summer of 1988, and the redevelopment of the Majestic and the Empire, put the project in jeopardy. In August of 1988 the theatre was purchased by the San Antonio Conservation Society.

The Aztec was the last downtown theatre to show first run movies. Also notable about the Aztec is the fact that it was at one time one of the few theatres to have its own symphony.

The Empire - The Empire is just around the corner from the Majestic, but it is much smaller. It ended its days as a movie house by showing adult films. It sat empty for almost ten years until the performing arts district became a reality. The building seats about 900 and will be used for chamber music and repertory theatre.

The Empire and the Majestic were redesigned to share many of the support facilities, such as dressing rooms, offices, and a music library. The restoration of the Empire is the second phase of the redevelopment of the new performing arts district.

The Texas - The Texas Theatre, designed by the Bollner Brothers, opened on December 18, 1926. (Remember, the first talking picture did not arrive until 1927.) One of the most important events in the history of the palace was the premiere of the film *Wings*, which was the first movie to win an Academy Award (see Wings - the Movie). The Texas was decorated in a wild West-rococo style and featured a plaster canopy that assisted the acoustics. The canopy, a Bollner Brothers trademark, was connected to the walls of a Spanish patio. At the center of the patio was a lone star which stood not for Texas, but was the symbol of the Publix Theatre chain.

The Texas also featured three balconies, the top being segregated seating. A third box office and a special concession stand were also provided for black patrons. The theatre also had a pipe organ, but it was removed from the theatre sometime around World War II. Like many other theatres of the era, its walls were adorned by murals. The Texas' walls featured the work of artist Jose Arpa.

The Texas sat over 2700 and, throughout its existence, it hosted a variety of entertainers from Bing Crosby and W. C. Fields to a number of rock bands. It was one of only two Bollner Brothers fantasy-type theatres left in existence, and conservationists felt the auditorium was worth fighting for.

Unfortunately, the Dallas developers felt differently. Republic Bank (which has gone through a few name changes and is now known as North Carolina National Bank of Texas) wanted to tear down the theatre to build a block-long office plaza. Conservationists wanted the theatre to be incorporated into the design and even offered their own plans. The out-of-town bank said a huge auditorium did not fit into its vision.

The bank offered a compromise by hiring the architectural firm of Ford, Powell, and Associates who would incorporate the facade of the old theatre into the new building. The San Antonio Conservation Society offered its own solution. First, it offered 12 million dollars to purchase the theatre. When the offer was refused, the society hired its own architect to draw up a new set of plans. The society commissioned noted preservationist Michael Graves, who designed a skyscraper that not only saved the theatre, but incorporated some of the Texas features into the new building. Once again, the Conservation Society's offer was turned down.

After a series of court battles and protests, the Texas Theatre finally was torn down. The facade was saved, but many felt the final solution was a poor compromise that served neither party's interests. The loss of the movie house has been intensified now that the Majestic and the Empire have been renovated. As the performing arts district becomes a reality, the loss of one of the crown jewels of Houston Street will be forever missed.

The Alameda - Officially known as the Alameda Theatre and International Building, it was built in 1949. The building, designed by architect Straus Nayfach, was built as a monument to Pan American unity. The building is known for its murals depicting the history of Texas and Mexico. It also has some interesting tile work on the inside and out. The theatre is located on Houston Street just west of the Majestic and until recently was showing Spanish language films.

The Cameo - Situated in the St. Paul's Square historic district, this theatre at one time mainly catered to a black audience. Since the square has been restored, the theatre has been used as a concert hall, a small performance hall, and a nightclub.

Other Downtown Theatres

When downtown was the only place for entertainment in San Antonio, it featured numerous theatres. Many started out by featuring live shows and then were later converted to movie palaces. Alamo Plaza features two movie houses. The Palace, located at 325 Alamo Plaza, was the first theatre built by the Santikos family. It closed in 1954. The Plaza theatre was located next to Joske's on the corner of Blum and Alamo Plaza in the Conroy Building. The theatre closed in 1939 when the building was bought by the department store in their quest to become the biggest store in the biggest state.

The State was another of the city's more prominent theatres. Located at 209 Main Avenue, it was closed in 1959. Houston Street was by far the most popular destination for moviegoers. It featured a slew of movie houses, including the Prince, the Rivoli, the Rialto (the first theatre bought by the Santikos family), the Pearl, the Orpheum, the Royal, the Princess, the Jewel, and the Star. Most of these closed during the early days of the Depression.

Suburban Theatres

What we now consider to be suburban theatres, those large ten plus screen complexes in loopland, are actually the second wave of suburban theatres. If you look hard enough, you can still find the remnants of the first wave. Though not as stunning as the downtown palaces, the theatres still had more atmosphere than most of today's complexes. Unfortunately, these neighborhood houses could not compete with the new suburban complexes and none of them continue to show first run movies.

The Broadway - The Broadway finished showing movies in the early '80s and later became the home of a bank. The old movie house is located in downtown Alamo Heights on Broadway across from H.E.B.

The Laurel - The Laurel is gone, torn down in 1986. The building was located south of Hildebrand on San Pedro. It was one of three local theatres to be designed by John Ebersol's company. The parking lot for the Laurel is used now for the faculty of Mark Twain Junior High.

The Olmos - The Olmos, located on San Pedro, tried valiantly to survive. It first became a second run theatre, then an arts movie house. Later it showed adult films. It has been remodeled now and is barely recognized as an old theatre. It is now the home of the San Antonio College of Medical and Dental Assistants.

The Guadalupe - The Guadalupe, originally known as the Progreso Theatre, was built in 1941 to host both movies and vaudeville performances. Located at the corner of Guadalupe and Brazos streets, the theatre was completely restored in 1984 to host a variety of community events. The theatre along with the adjacent Plaza Guadalupe have become the focal point for revitalizing the west side.

The Uptown - The Uptown was sold to St. Anne's Catholic Church and is now a gym for the school. The front of the theatre on Fredricksburg Rd. has been closed up and is no longer recognizable, but if you step inside, the old building reveals its former self. The gym floor is surrounded by the stage and theatre trim. The lobby is now used for storage.

The Wonder - The first mall theatre was located in the parking lot of Wonderland Mall (now Crossroads) near the highway interchange. The theatre was closed and the building was torn down in 1987, when a new theatre opened inside the mall.

The Woodlawn - This suburban showplace was also designed by John Ebersol's company. It sits in a plaza along with shops and a bowling alley. The Woodlawn on Fredericksburg Rd. has a place in history because it was the site for the premiere of *The Alamo*. The theatre was also the launching pad for the play *Alice in Wonderland*. It has tried its hand as a second run house, an arts house, a concert hall, and a church. The bowling alley is now a ballroom available for rent.

The Josephine - The Josephine, located at the corner of Josephine and St. Mary's, ended its career as a movie house by showing adult movies. The theatre sat vacant for several years, and in 1988 it was reclaimed as the home of the Alamo Community Theatre. One of the theatre's saving graces was its location. When the theatre closed, the neighborhood was on the downturn. But as fortune would have it, St. Mary's Street became "The Strip," and the theatre found itself at the end of one of the most exciting streets in San Antonio.

How many of these other suburban theatres do you remember? Sunset, Star, Highland, Harlandale, National, and Zaragoza (Spanish).

Drive-Ins

The Mission Drive-In on Roosevelt is the city's last open-air theatre. At one time, San Antonio was the host to several such establishments. Many were at the edge of town and now have been replaced by shopping centers and apartments. Others were converted to auto salvage yards, junkyards, or other such businesses. How many of these do you remember?

Alamo	1428 Austin Highway
Circle 81	New Laredo Highway & Zarzamora
Fred. Road	3600 Fredricksburg
Parkair	1301 Goliad
Kelly	Taft & Frio City Road
Lackland	3500 S.W. Military
Rigsby	Rigsby & Military
S.A. Twin	Highway 90 East
South Loop 13	S.W. Military Drive
San Pedro	Bitters at 281
Trail	Military & Roosevelt
Varsity	Culebra & Bandera
Bandera Road	Bandera and Loop 13 (now Loop 410)

The River Walk

Next to the Alamo, the River Walk is the city's most recognizable landmark. The River Walk generates so much economic power, not to mention civic pride, that almost every city in Texas has tried to copy it or is developing similar plans. Unfortunately, most of these plans are destined to fail, because developers and city planners who try to copy the River Walk know little about the history of the attraction and are destined to discover the same pitfalls as San Antonians did decades earlier.

The San Antonio River - 1920s

The San Antonio River was not always a source of affection for the city's downtown merchants—especially on September 9, 1921, when a major flood dumped nine feet of water on Houston Street. The water was up to the second level of the Gunter Hotel and washed out merchants up and down the street. It was the twelfth flood to hit the city since 1819, and city fathers felt the need to implement a flood control plan.

Everybody realized a need for some type of system to prevent the damage which occurred every time it flooded. A dam was proposed for Olmos Basin. Some engineers proposed cutting a new channel for the river and eliminating the big bend portion of the river. The eliminated portion could be paved over for parking or possibly another thoroughfare. This plan was supported by many on the river because an extra street would give them an additional street storefront.

The River Walk Proposal

Three parties are responsible for the idea of the River Walk. The first was a young architect named Robert Hugman. Hugman developed an idea whereby the river banks on the big bend area would be transformed into a park-like area with public access and an area of commerce known as the shops of Aragon and Romula. The idea was years ahead of its time; it was decades before urban renewal projects and festival market places were being proposed. The River Walk would feature shops offering food from around the world. The banks would be clear of litter and debris. Merchants would clean up the backs of their property and cease to use the river as an alley and a dumping ground. Hugman proposed this then-radical idea in 1929. His plan was nothing more than a vision for six years, until local hotel owner Jack White began to look for a way to attract more tourists to San Antonio.

White organized a River Beautification Board to promote the idea of a river walk. Landowners who had river access pledged over $30,000, but getting money from the city was difficult. By now the Depression was in full swing, and money was tight. After numerous defeats with the city council, White finally managed to convince the city government to form a special San Antonio River Improvement District. The district consisted of one hundred and seven people who lived on or owned property with riverfront access. The group voted a special tax for themselves, in 1938, that would establish $75,000 for river improvement. It was then that the Works Project Administration became interested in the River Walk as a way of putting Depression-era men back to work. The WPA kicked in $325,000 toward the project.

One more group assisted in making the project a reality. The San Antonio Conservation Society took city fathers on a boat trip down the river to illustrate the possibilities. A puppet show entitled "The Goose that Laid the Golden Egg," which demonstrated the economic possibilities of a river walk, was presented to the city council. The Society was quite young at the time and had nowhere near the influence

117

it has today; nevertheless, the women of the Conservation Society were instrumental in swaying public opinion. The effort to beautify the River Walk became the first of many victories for the organization.

Construction of the River Walk

Ground breaking ceremonies for the project took place March 25, 1939, ten years after Hugman made the proposal. Jack White, who would later become mayor, was given the honor of being the first to dip the golden shovel. Robert Hugman was hired as the architect by the city.

One of the first things that needed to be done was the cleaning and deepening of the river channel. During the dredging, workers uncovered wagon wheels, cannonballs, guns, and a host of other items. Floodgates were also built to cut off the big bend area from the rest of the river channel during high water. These gates effectively cut off the shops and restaurants from the high water during flooding.

Few people realize the effort involved in Hugman's design. Thirty-one stairwells were designed to give the public access to the river from the street level. No two were alike. The first completed stairwell was made of cedar posts and went from the Crockett Street bridge to the river's east bank.

Careful attention was also paid to landscaping the River Walk. A large number of small trees and shrubs were stored by local nurseries until they could be replanted. Trees that had their roots uncovered by the dredging were treated with the utmost care. Crutches were built to aid many large trees during the construction, and tree surgery was performed on many large trees. Over 11,000 trees and shrubs were planted by workmen. The construction effort attracted attention from across the country. Celebrated columnist Ernie Pyle visited the site in 1939 and wrote an article entitled "An American Venice in the Making, San Antonio Is Doing Tricks With Its Winding Downtown River" for the Scripps-Howard newspaper syndicate.

The project was completed on March 14, 1941. The effort cost $430,000. Seventeen thousand feet of sidewalks were completed. Eleven thousand cubic yards of masonry and 3,200 cubic yards of concrete were used.

Unfortunately, Hugman had been fired a year earlier. The young architect got caught in a bureaucratic shuffle over materials being sent to the La Villita construction site rather than the River Walk. A meeting of the river board released Hugman without benefit of a hearing. Officially, it was announced that the visionary architect was released because he failed to hire a landscape architect and because many of his cost estimates were off base. Hugman was devastated by the dismissal. The man who was known as the father of the River Walk was often bypassed when credit for the project was given. It was not until 1978 that Hugman was finally recognized for his contributions. That year the bells were finally added to the Arneson River Theatre and were dedicated to the River Walk's originator.

The River Walk's Troublesome Early Years

The River Walk was anything but an instant success. During World War II there was a shortage of labor to maintain the park-like settings. Many businesses resumed their practice of dumping garbage in the water and using the river as an alley. Vandalism and petty crime became common occurrences. Poor lighting made the River Walk a dangerous place after dark. For many years the Army declared the River Walk off-limits to military personnel. One air force colonel, who returned to San Antonio in the '80s remarked that when he was a young airman stationed in town, the River Walk was a good place to "get rolled."

The first restaurant to open on the river was Casa Rio, in 1946, by A. F. Beyer. He was joined on the river level by Robert Hugman who opened his architect office next to the Commerce Street bridge. Both were the subject of a few raised eyebrows. Who would want to open a business on the river? They would be flooded out for sure.

During the 1950s, interest in the River Walk was renewed when the city and the Chamber of Commerce commissioned a study to determine a proper future for the river. In 1962 the River Walk District and the River Walk Advisory Commission were formed. With the upcoming World's Fair, things began to change.

The River Walk, 1968 to Present

Hemisfair '68 is often credited with giving the River Walk its second life. With the upcoming showcase around the corner, the city appropriated $500,000 to improve it. The Chamber of Commerce formed the Paseo Del Rio Association from business people who had a stake in the river. The river was extended east toward the new convention center, the first addition in over twenty years. A first-class hotel, the Hilton Palacio del Rio, was built on the river and was soon joined by La Mansion Del Rio. Thousands of tourists who came to town discovered the River Walk for the first time.

Soon more restaurants began to open and other hotels were added. The "Shops of Aragon and Romula" that Robert Hugman once envisioned were finally becoming a reality. The River Walk continued to expand. While it once ended just after the Tower Life Building, it now extends all the way to the King William District. With the construction of the Hyatt Regency, the Paseo Del Rio was connected to Alamo Plaza via a series of waterfalls. In 1988 Rivercenter, a massive shopping complex built around an extension of the river, was opened. The new downtown mall has been one of the most successful ventures because it has lured suburbanites back downtown.

During the 1980s, the River Walk became Texas' second leading tourist attraction, right behind the Alamo.

The Future

No one knows for certain what the future holds for the River Walk. Plans have been discussed to extend it further—all the way to Brackenridge Park to the north and towards the missions to the south. Many people doubt that the river will ever fall into disrepair again. After a slow start, the River Walk now generates millions of dollars for the city.

A careful Paseo del Rio association keeps a watchful eye on future development. When City Public Service wanted to add three stories of office space atop a downtown parking garage, they were required to stagger the building to allow sunlight to pass below. The association also keeps tabs on merchants to keep obtrusive signs and loud music from disturbing the tranquil setting. As the River Walk enters its fifth decade, its popularity continues to grow by leaps and bounds. Local visionaries are dedicated to keeping the Paseo Del Rio a unique urban oasis.

Read More About It:

Lomax, Louise. *San Antonio's River*. San Antonio: The Naylor Company, 1948.

Zunker, Vernon G. *A Dream Come True: Robert Hugman and San Antonio's River Walk*. San Antonio: 1983.

Acequias and the Aqueduct

If ever there was a city whose past depended on water, San Antonio is it. Of course, one could argue that many great cities sprung up around massive bays or powerful rivers, and that San Antonio had neither. But the abundant waters from the Edwards Aquifer made life possible for the last three centuries. It was the river and the lush vegetation that surrounded it that first attracted the Spanish to this place.

In the early 1700s, the Franciscan priests who established the missions built ditches to supply themselves and their fields with water. These ditches, known as acequias, were engineering marvels. They had to drop one inch for every 100 feet for the water to flow. Perhaps the biggest problem was creating an aqueduct to carry water over the Piedras creek bed. It is the only Spanish-built aqueduct in the United States.

Long after the mission had faded, the acequias still existed and served water throughout the city. In the 1800s the ditches supplied water to beautiful gardens of homes which were lucky enough to be near them. The prominent German families built their homes along the Acequia Madre or the Alamo Ditch. Many of the early roads in San Antonio followed the ditches; in fact, Main Street in downtown San Antonio was originally known as Acequia Street. The acequias also became dumping grounds and provided a crude sewer system, not to mention a breeding ground for typhoid and cholera. In 1879 George Brackenridge's Water Works Company began supplying water to the city and most of the acequias dried up.

Small pieces of the acequias can still be found in the downtown area. The Alamo grounds features a ditch. Sections of restored acequias can be found in Hemisfair Park next to the children's playground and in front of the new

Justice Center on Main Plaza. Perhaps the best place to view them is at Mission San Juan Capistrano on the far south side. Here the water still flows, and you can follow it along the river, through the woods, to the aqueduct, which still exists today.

Both the aqueduct and the acequias are National Historic Civil Engineering monuments. The aqueduct, built before this country was formed, still works today and is perhaps the most forgotten historic site in the city. It is well worth a trip to see this engineering marvel that time forgot. To get there by car, take Mission Road south from SW Military Drive past Stinson Field Airport. The road changes to Ashley, but continue on to Espada Rd. Turn right and you should see it at about 200 yards. The aqueduct feeds water to the acequia on to Mission Espada. You could follow the acequia on to the mission, but this is not recommended because you would be trespassing on private property. Instead, a short drive down Espada Rd. will take you there.

Another interesting site just north of the Aqueduct is the Espada Dam on the San Antonio River. The dam was built between 1731 and 1745 and has stood for over 200 years, withstanding many significant floods. The dam is an engineering marvel because it is curved the wrong way. The dam was constructed with goats milk mixed with the mortar to make it waterproof. To view the dam, turn south on Mission Parkway just off Southwest Military Drive.

San Antonio's Most Important Acequias

1. The Alamo Madre or Mother Ditch
2. The Upper and Lower Labor Ditches
3. The Apalatchie
4. The Alazan
5. The Flores Street Ditch
6. The Pajalahe or Concepcion Ditch
7. The San Pedro Ditch

San Pedro Park

Located across the street from San Antonio College, San Pedro Park has a special place in local history. This often neglected piece of city property is the second oldest park in the United States. In 1729 King Phillip V of Spain declared through his viceroy in Mexico that the headwaters of the San Pedro become public land or "elido." Only the park known as Boston Commons is older.

The springs were discovered on April 13, 1709, by Father Isidro Felix De Espinosa's expedition. It was he who named the springs. At the time, the water flow was so powerful that many mistook San Pedro Creek for the San Antonio River. For years the area known today as San Pedro Park was a popular camping area for travelers. The military often used the area for its troops. Soldiers camped there in 1846 during the Mexican American War. During the Civil War, the Confederate army used the grounds as a POW camp.

After the Civil War, the city of San Antonio leased control of the park to private citizens who would sell concessions, book entertainment, and provide for its upkeep. These private operators built lakes, rented boats, had a small zoo, and provided gas lights for nighttime activities. The park's heyday began in 1874, when Colonel Augustus Belknap built a streetcar line from downtown out to the park. The first cars were mule drawn and ran from 6 A.M. to midnight. The cost of the ride was 6 ½ cents. A Museum of Natural History opened in 1885 at the park, the city's first museum. The grotto (located behind the library) was constructed in the 1880s and was originally designed as summer quarters, which were very much in vogue at the time.

In 1891 the city assumed control of all its parks, and San Pedro Park continued to improve. Balloon rides were the fashion of the day and, for a price, a park patron could experience the thrill of a lifetime. The park was so popular that just south of San Pedro a private facility called Electric Park was opened.

Meanwhile, improvements continued at San Pedro Park. The city's first zoo opened there in 1910. In 1922 a swimming pool was built in the park, the first in the city. The pool was built on the lake bed, and a bridge that spanned the lake was incorporated into the design of the modern pool. The spring water fed the pool and flushed it out every eight hours. In 1929 San Antonio Little Theatre opened in the northwest corner of the park. The outside of the theatre was a replica of the old Market House downtown, which had been torn down years earlier. That same year, the city's first branch library opened at the park.

A girl cools herself under the spillway of the old San Pedro pool.

By now the park was in decline. Although the pool was very popular and new at the time, Brackenrige Park was now a more popular park. Even the zoo had to relocate to the newer facility. In addition, increased water demands severely hampered the flow of water from the springs. By the 1940s the water flow was so poor it was no longer capable of cleaning the pool, and the facility had to be closed.

In 1954 Howard E. Butt gave the city the financial backing to build a new pool at the park. This pool is the one that stands today: rectangular, surrounded by a fence, with huge tanks that take water from the city supply rather than the springs. Although the pool is heavily used and functional, it is not nearly as picturesque as its predecessor.

The park continued to decline for many years; most San Antonians did not even realize its history or its proud past. In the 1980s awareness of the park's history began to rise. New playground equipment was built with help from the neighborhood. Active citizens raised money to clean up the grounds and restore some of the gardens. Proposals have been brought forth to rebuild the old pool. As the park closes in on its third century of life, it is finally receiving the respect it deserves.

Travis Park

The third oldest park in America is located in San Antonio. It is no larger than a city block, and it is located downtown at the corner of Navarro and Travis. The greenspace, known as Travis Park, is located across from the St. Anthony Hotel.

The land for the park was donated by Samuel Maverick. Maverick was the only Alamo defender to survive the infamous battle. He left the compound a few days before the siege to sign the Texas Declaration of Independence. He later established a home near the Alamo, at what is now the site of the Gibbs Building (corner of Houston and Alamo). The land which is now Travis Park was his orchard.

In the 1950s there was a push to convert the park into a parking garage, even though the deed to the city specified that the land only be used as a park. There was a proposal to build an underground parking garage and leave the park intact. The Maverick family filed suit to protect the park. A great granddaughter of Samuel Maverick, who was in the sixth grade at the time, organized a letter-writing campaign of school children to save the park. The sixth grader was Marjo Rodgers, who later became the first director of the San Antonio Park Partners.

Though the park was saved from the bulldozer, it was not saved from the many undesirable characters who began to frequent the area. The facility became a haven for prostitutes. In the early 1980s the city refurbished the park, and with the advent of better lighting and increased police protection, the city block became a favorite among those who live, work, play, and pray in the downtown area. Travis Park is now the site of the JazzAlive concert series each year, as well as the city's brown bag lunch program.

San Antonio's Rail History

San Antonio, like other Texas cities, relied heavily on the rail system in its early days. The first train chugged into the city on February 16, 1877. The Galveston, Harrisburg, and San Antonio Railway connected the Sunset Line to the city. That railway later became the Southern Pacific. The advent of the railroads changed San Antonio forever. The city was difficult to reach and was made up of mostly German, Spanish, and Mexican descendants. The rails brought people of different cultures and different religions for the first time. The first influx of Anglo Americans and people who followed the Protestant religions came after the rails.

The first Protestant churches were soon built to serve the new San Antonians, and the new churches brought new ministers who frowned on the rough and rowdy traditions of the frontier town.

Many San Antonians thought the new railroad meant new wealth; however, few people got rich off the trains. The few who profited were mainly German merchants who had businesses before the train rolled into town. The rails did force the town to modernize. With the influx of new people, the old system of acequias supplying water was inadequate. A new water works was quickly developed.

The age of heavy rail use has passed, but San Antonio is fortunate because two of its main terminals are still in existence, with many of the period buildings surrounding them still intact.

The Southern Pacific Station

Located in St. Paul's Square (1174 E. Commerce), the Southern Pacific Station is the city's only remaining active passenger terminal. The building was completed in 1903 in a Mission Melange style. The interior has been beautifully restored and boasts a beautiful rose window on the south side of the building featuring the seal of the state of Texas. The rose window on the north side featured the emblem of the Southern Pacific Lines, but it no longer exists.

The building is the home to Amtrak service in San Antonio and, to the Texan, a seven-car dinner express that sends travelers on a four-hour trip down the rails and back in time to a place when traveling and dining meant more than prepackaged airplane food.

The Southern Pacific terminal can be seen from your car just off I-37, across the highway from Hemisfair Plaza. But this terminal is best enjoyed by stopping, parking in the old brick parking lot, and walking through the terminal and the neighborhood. The outside of the building has yet to be restored, but the surrounding St. Paul's Square has been transformed back to its earlier splendor. The east side of the terminal features a long covered area for waiting passengers, which is a favorite of this writer. By strolling through the area, one can easily imagine himself in any time period.

The free parking at the train station is also convenient for downtowners—for a dime you can take a trolley ride throughout downtown.

The Missouri Pacific Terminal

Long known as the forgotten terminal, this beautiful building received a new life in 1988. The structure sits at the west end of Houston Street in the Cattlemen's Square area and was designed by Harvey L. Page (who was also the architect for the Frost Building on Houston Street). It was built in 1907. Originally, it was the terminal for the International and Great Northern Railway (whose name is engraved around the stained glass window). It later became the Missouri Pacific Terminal in the 1930s.

The dome on the terminal was covered with copper and was topped with a famous Indian. The railway closed the terminal in 1970 when the railroad discontinued the route from Texarkana to Laredo, and the building fell into great disrepair. The windows were broken, the copper stripped from the roof, the neighborhood totally collapsed, and it became a haven for day laborers, drunks, and prostitutes.

In 1982 the famous Indian was stolen from the top of the dome, and the terminal continued to rot away. Some experts feared the building would be lost forever if a plan was not developed to revitalize and reuse the building. There were many suggestions, including making it into a farmers market, the main library, a science and transportation museum, a restaurant, or a city court building. The City Employee Credit Union was finally able to come up with a viable plan for the building and negotiated the sale of the structure (which had always been a major stumbling block) for $7 million. The old Mopac terminal officially became the headquarters for the city credit union in the summer of 1988. The credit union spent 3.2 million dollars restoring the terminal, complete with a new copper dome. The transformation has been incredible and took the efforts of many people. The stained glass windows were faithfully reproduced by Joe Juarez and Diane Court of Black's Art Glass Studio. The wood framing for the copper roof took three months alone to replace.

As for the Indian, he eventually returned to his perch. The statue was found on Good Friday in 1982. The hollow statue was originally believed to be solid cast iron, which made many wonder how the roof could support it and how someone could walk off with it. The Indian was found in a field near the station, but his bow had been shattered, all his feathers were shot off, his right leg was broken off, and his butt was caved in. Lucille Pratte spearheaded a five-year effort to have the Indian restored. Blacksmith artist Alan Lewis of Medina Valley Forge spent four months and $4,500 restoring the statue. The 15-foot, 200-pound statue was brought home to its familiar perch on April 21, 1988.

City Hall

San Antonio's city hall is one of the oldest in Texas. It was built between 1888 and 1891 in the middle of Military Plaza. The construction of the facility ended the open-air market and the public gatherings which were popular there for almost a century.

The original design of the hall is strikingly different from its present appearance. A St. Louis architect designed a three-story building with a domed octagonal clock tower in the center. Two of the corners supported conical towers while the other corners had mansard rook towers. One of the entrances had a two-story portico and a balcony for the second floor.

City Hall before the fourth floor was added.

When a fourth floor was added in 1927, the towers and the portico were removed, leaving the building without its most striking features. Today a discriminating eye will be able to determine how the original corner towers fit onto the three-story version of city hall.

Hotels

"Every Texan has two homes, his own and San Antonio."   *J. Frank Dobie*

Visitors to San Antonio (or locals who are looking for a romantic weekend) have a clear choice when looking for downtown lodging. They can go for historic elegance or opt for striking modern beauty. Most of the city's classic old-line hotels have been faithfully restored and are still offering the type of service they have always been famous for.

The Historic Hotels

The St. Anthony

Named in honor of the city's patron saint, San Antonio de Padua, the St. Anthony is both a Texas and National Historical Landmark. Built in 1909, across from Travis Park, the hotel was an instant success, and soon a second wing and three more stories were added. In 1936 railroad tycoon R. W. Morrison purchased the hotel and made it his goal to make the St. Anthony one of the nation's greatest hotels.

Morrison built a third wing in 1941 and also purchased many of the hotel's antiques and fine works of art. Paintings include those of Remington, Cartier, De Young, and James Ferdinand McCann. Perhaps the most famous antique is the rosewood and bronze Steinway piano located in the lobby. The piano was purchased from the Russian embassy in Paris when it was selling assets to pay its war debts.

Throughout the years, the St. Anthony has hosted such famous guests as Franklin D. Roosevelt, Ronald Reagan, Bob Hope, Princess Grace of Monaco, and John Wayne. A suite is named in honor of Wayne, who was a frequent guest.

Samuel Gompers, founder of the American Federation of Labor, died at the hotel after returning from an international labor conference in Mexico.

The hotel is an innovator in the hotel industry. It was the first air-conditioned hotel in the world, the first with a now common drive-up registration, and the first to use automatic doors. In 1981 the St. Anthony went through a 27-million-dollar restoration, ensuring that the hotel will serve many more generations of visitors.

The Gunter

Another downtown hotel listed on the National Register of Historic Places, the Gunter was built in 1909 and was the city's largest building at that time. The Gunter was the city's only steel structure and featured such innovations as a central heating system, four elevators, and complete baths in 70 percent of the rooms. In 1917 a ninth floor was added, and three more floors were added in 1927.

Mae West at the Gunter Hotel.

Located on the corner of St. Mary's and Houston streets, the hotel has long been a center for cattlemen visiting the city. In 1921 San Antonio's most disastrous flood dumped six feet of water into the lobby. In 1985 the Gunter was restored at a cost of 25 million dollars.

The Menger

The city's most historic hotel, located next to the Alamo, is the Menger, which originally started out as a brewery. The Menger has hosted presidents, movie stars, and poets. Teddy Roosevelt recruited his Rough Riders in the hotel lobby. (For more about the Menger see "Eleven Facts About the Menger Hotel" in the San Antonio Lists at the back of the book.)

The city also features some of the most unique restorations in the hotel industry. The Emily Morgan Hotel was previously a medical building. La Mansion Del Rio was built on the old downtown campus of St. Mary's University. The Fairmount Hotel, one of the city's finest, was once located four blocks away. In 1985 it set a record as the largest building ever moved. (More about these hotels is written elsewhere in the book.) Visitors may also want to check out the recently restored Crockett Hotel, nestled on a romantic corner behind the Alamo and next to Rivercenter.

The Modern Hotels

The Hilton Palacio Del Rio

When it was constructed, the Hilton was the first hotel to be built in downtown San Antonio in almost thirty years. It was built to accommodate visitors to Hemisfair '68. The hotel was the first in the world to be completed using modular construction techniques and was finished in record time. Six rooms were cast at a time. Each room was equipped with a bathroom and furniture (including a Bible in the end table) before it was added to the building.

Guests were allowed to check into their rooms before the entire hotel was completed. Some guests checked into their rooms before they were added on, and they received a once-in-a-lifetime ride, as a crane hoisted room and guest atop the foundation.

The Hilton was completed in time for the World's Fair and was the first in a new wave of construction. With the advent of Hemisfair came a new convention center and a rejuvenated River Walk. San Antonio was soon rediscovered by tourists. A new Marriott Hotel was built next to the convention center on the River Walk extension. A Hyatt Hotel was added on Lasoya Street, featuring a stream running through the lobby, which for the first time connected the River Walk and the Alamo (the state's #1 and #2 tourist attractions) via an attractive walkway.

With the advent of Rivercenter came a new Marriott with 1000 rooms, by far the city's largest hotel. The twin faux towers were added as a tribute to the Tower Life Building, which for many years was the city's largest structure. As the city rolls into the 1990s, there is talk of further expanding the downtown lodging industry, as San Antonio becomes a bigger tourist mecca.

The Road Into Town

During the 1950s and 1960s, when the automobile was king and the open road ruled, San Antonio featured a thriving motel industry. When interstate highways were added, many of these motels were closed or converted into other businesses.

Austin Highway brought in motorists from the north before I-35 was built, Fredericksburg Road was the main way into town from the west before I-10, and old Highway 90 brought in visitors from the southwest. When traveling down these roads, a discerning eye can spot numerous old hotels, service stations, and drive-ins that are relics of a time past.

Jefferson High School

When it was completed in 1932, Jefferson High School was years ahead of its time. Built on the edge of town (the school is now firmly surrounded by the city), the school cost the unheard-of sum of $1,500,000. The Spanish-Moorish design came complete with many amenities new to the San Antonio School District. It has two gymnasiums, built-in lockers, tile floors, wrought iron balconies, fountains, a 2000-seat auditorium, and a prominent tower that overlooks the campus.

An aerial view of Jefferson High School in the early '30s.

The school was such a masterpiece that *Life* magazine featured it in its March 7, 1939, issue. The Lasso Girls drill team (who later that year would perform at the New York World's Fair) graced the cover, and the popular publication proclaimed Jefferson to be "the new elite in American high schools." The magazine boasted the school's three orchestras, its top-notch ROTC drill teams, and its unique courses, such as radio broadcasting (which later would produce prominent alumnus Bruce Hathaway, well-known San Antonio disc jockey). The school, located on the "Texas Prairie," was said to have more playing fields than many Texas colleges.

Two movies were filmed at the school: *High School* in 1937 and *Texas Girl* in 1939. For years it was a tradition for students to view the films each year in the school's spacious auditorium. In 1983 the student council had the school declared a Texas Historical Landmark, and it was listed in the National Register of Historic Places.

The Municipal Auditorium

One of the city's finest public buildings is the Municipal Auditorium. Built in 1926, the vintage Moorish building won an award for its architect, Atlee B. Ayres, from the American Institute of Architects. It was built at a cost of 1.5 million dollars and has hosted such dignitaries as Richard Nixon, Lyndon Johnson, Bob Hope, Will Rogers, Martin and Lewis, Al Jolson, Elvis Presley, Eleanor Roosevelt, Pope John Paul II, and comedians Jay Leno, Michael O' Roarke, and Mark Louis.

The auditorium was built as a memorial to those who served in World War I. As a memorial, it was quite impressive; however, as a money maker, it was a white elephant.

Municipal Auditorium during the 1929 Christmas season.

The facility is a shining jewel in the city's crown, but for many years it was treated as a poor stepchild. It was never remodeled, and over the years it fell into disrepair. In 1962 Mayor McAllister called the building a "disgrace to the city" and suggested the city convert it to a convention center at a cost of five million dollars. When the new convention center was built in Hemisfair Plaza, the auditorium fell into its role as a second class hall. It became the home for wrestling and rock concerts.

On January 6, 1979, flames ripped through the building. The roof and the old pipe organ were destroyed. Only the outer shell and the stage (which was saved by the sprinkling system) remained. At first arson was suspected, but later it was discovered that a cigarette was the cause of the fire. The building sat in its semidestroyed state for three years. Some wanted it renovated into a home for the symphony. Others hoped the building would become a media production center. Many remembered the squalor of the auditorium's final years and hoped that the building would be torn down. They argued that because of the convention center, the Municipal Auditorium was no longer needed.

After much debate, the city decided to rebuild the facility. In retrospect, the decision was the right one. The facility reopened in February, 1986. The renovation has been spectacular, and the city has forgotten the debate that once surrounded the auditorium.

Old Places, New Uses

One of the unique qualities of San Antonio is its penchant for finding new uses for old buildings. The old Mopac train terminal is now the City Employees Credit Union. The Broadway Theatre is now a bank. The Casino Club building is now an apartment building. The following are further examples of old buildings that have been put to new uses.

The H.E.B. Headquarters - Formerly the U.S. Arsenal

This massive complex on Durango Street and Main was originally built in 1858 as an arsenal for the U.S. Army. It replaced the Alamo, which the Army was using at the time for storage. Water was originally brought to the compound by one of the various acequias that existed in San Antonio at the time. During the Civil War, the armory was used by Confederate soldiers. In 1865 it was returned to the U.S. Army and supplied Texas troops. Additional buildings were built on the site in 1916 and 1933.

In 1949 the arsenal closed. Some of the buildings were used for many years by the Marine Corps Reserve, but for the most part the buildings sat vacant. In 1984 the South Texas grocery store chain H.E.B. began renovation on the complex for use as its new headquarters. H.E.B. did a remarkable job in its renovation, as can be witnessed by looking at the old Marine Corps Reserve building adjacent to the H.E.B. property which was not refinished. A walk along the River Walk in the King William District gives you an excellent view of the restored property. The designers were sympathetic to the neighborhood that surrounds the headquarters; instead of a being an eyesore to those living next to the complex, the headquarters was designed to blend in with the surrounding homes and the adjacent River Walk. It is interesting to note that a grocery store chain chose downtown San Antonio as its headquarters, but downtown San Antonio is devoid of any grocery store.

The only building in the complex that was left untouched was a thick concrete building in the middle of the grounds that was used to store explosives. Because of the thickness of the walls, the architects decided to leave the building in its original state.

Across Main Street are some other structures that were part of the original arsenal. The Commander's House is now used as a Senior Citizen Recreation Center, while some others were retained for government use.

The San Antonio Museum of Art - Formerly the Lone Star Brewery

Perhaps San Antonio's greatest reclamation is the former Lone Star Brewery. No other building has received as much national press as the Lone Star Brewery conversion. Located on 200 W. Jones on the banks of the San Antonio River, the brewery was opened in 1903 by beer king Adolphus Busch. Busch brought architects from the finest schools in Germany to design the buildings. The Lone Star Brewing Association originally produced beer under the Alamo and Erlanger labels. By 1905 it was the largest brewery in Texas, dwarfing the numerous small German brewers in the area at the time. The glory days for the building ended in 1921 with the advent of prohibition. For a time, a soft drink named Tango was bottled there. Later the structure became the home of the Lone Star Ice Company and, later still, a cotton mill. After prohibition, the Lone Star label was bought by Harry Jersig for a new brewery being built on the south side.

The building went through a variety of uses and was gutted by fire before the Museum Association bought the complex for a mere $375,000 in 1972. At the time, the Witte Museum was exhibiting both art and natural history. The association planned to eventually move all the art exhibits to the new museum. On July 14, 1977, the brewery officially became the San Antonio Museum of Art and was christened by Mayor Lila Cockrell with a longneck bottle. It took three years to completely renovate the old bottling facility into a showplace. The two towers were connected by a spectacular glass walkway, and few of the building's outstanding features have been altered. From the outside, it still resembles a brewery.

Listed on the National Register of Historic Places, the San Antonio Museum of Art has won numerous awards for its restoration. Its two and one-half acres of riverfront property and its variety of unused buildings give the old brewery an exciting future in the art world.

The Hertzberg Circus Museum -
Formerly the San Antonio Public Library

In 1902 Andrew Carnegie donated $50,000 to the city for a new library. Land was donated by Mrs. Caroline Kampmann at the corner of Market and Presa. By the 1920s the building had become too small, and a new library was built on the same site and completed on August 1, 1930. The outside of the newer building is framed with quotes from some of America's most noted scholars. Today the old building is an annex to the new main library, but it is better known as the Hertzberg Circus Museum.

The museum is named after Harry Hertzberg, a local attorney, civic leader, and state senator. Hertzberg, an avid circus fan, began his collection in the 1920s. Many of the items were donated to Hertzberg by visiting circus performers who would often dine with him and his wife as they were passing through town. After his death in 1940, his collection was donated to the public library.

The collection includes over 20,000 items, many donated by circuses that currently visit the area. The museum's collection is today recognized as one of the most significant collections in the United States. It includes:

The oldest coach in existence, that once belonged to forty-inch-tall Tom Thumb

An ornate Gentry Bros. Circus parade wagon

A miniature circus that took thirteen years to build

Photos from Big Top stars and from Buffalo Bill's Wild West Show

Over 1000 circus books, including many rare titles

The museum is run by the city and is open to the public. There is no admission charge.

La Mansion Hotel - Formerly St. Mary's College

St. Mary's University on the city's northwest side had its modest beginnings in 1852 on the banks of the San Antonio River. Four Marianists Brothers from the Society of Mary came to San Antonio and opened St. Mary's Institute on August 25, 1852, above a livery shop on the southwest corner of Military Plaza. A permanent home, which is now part of La Mansion Hotel, was begun on March 1, 1853. It was once the largest building complex in the city. The school originally was for boys only and did not become completely coed until 1963.

The school grew quickly and expanded out to its present site in Woodlawn Hills in 1894, offering instruction in grades five through fourteen. The Woodlawn campus was known as St. Louis College and was located far outside the reaches of the city. Students had to take a bus to the corner of Woodlawn and Cincinnati and walk "the longest mile in Texas" to reach the school. The downtown facility was known as St. Mary's Academy (a high school for boys, which moved in 1932 to North Main and became Central Catholic High School) and St. Mary's College. The building housed St. Mary's Law School from 1934 to 1966, before they left downtown for the suburban location. The school is the only local college to serve the community for over 115 consecutive years and has educated eight San Antonio mayors.

In 1968 the River Hotel Company opened a hotel in the old school just in time to house Hemisfair visitors. It was one of only two major hotels to be built in downtown in the last fifty years. The building retained the style of the old college. If you walk into the courtyard, you can easily identify the old schoolhouse. La Mansion Del Rio has been designated a Texas historic site and has received a San Antonio

Conservation Society award. The main dining room in the hotel is named Las Canarias after the original Canary Islanders who founded the city.

The South Texas Regional Blood Bank - Formerly the YWCA

This historic building, located on the corner of McCullough and Broadway, was originally the home of the Young Women's Christian Association. The building was finished in 1915 and featured a horseshoe shape that included a courtyard. The structure was designed by local architect Atlee B. Ayres. The building took two years to build.

The Blood Bank took over occupancy of the building in the mid-1980s. The new tenants left many of the important features of the building intact. The horseshoe courtyard was enclosed with a glass atrium to provide extra indoor space and create a unique mix of nostalgia and modernity. The gymnasium has been carpeted over for office space and the swimming pool has been filled in. The Blood Bank building is an excellent example of how a historic building can be adapted and reused while preserving the integrity of the structure.

The Plaza San Antonio Hotel's Conference Center - Formerly the German-English School

The Plaza San Antonio Hotel on the corner of Durango and South Alamo Street utilizes one of the oldest school buildings in the city for its conference center. The structure, across S. Alamo from Beethoven Hall, was originally a school for the children of German intellectuals who lived in the Little Rhine section of the city. The school was built in 1859 by Johann H. Kampmann (who also built the Menger and the Lone Star Brewery). A third building was added in 1869.

The school was incorporated as the German-English School of San Antonio and modeled after the Gymnasium system of Germany. The institution had two principles: one, no religion was to be taught, and two, both German and English were to be equally emphasized. The curriculum and discipline were stiff. The school, facing financial difficulties and an improved public education system, closed in 1897.

The property was bought by Hilda and F. Groos, who later sold it to George W. Brackenridge. In 1903 Brackenridge deeded the grounds to the San Antonio Independent School District, who opened it up as Brackenridge Elementary. From 1923 to 1925 it was Page Junior High School. In 1926 it became the home of San Antonio College.

When SAC moved to its new home on San Pedro in 1951, the building was left vacant and fell into disrepair. In 1968 Hemisfair rescued the building from destruction and used it for office space.

After Hemisfair, the Four Seasons Hotel was built on the corner of Durango and South Alamo and incorporated the old school into a conference center. The Four Seasons chain sold out to Plaza San Antonio in the mid-1980s, continuing the tradition of the German-English School.

The Southwest Craft Center - Formerly the Ursuline Academy

The Ursuline Academy in San Antonio began in downtown San Antonio in 1851, when seven nuns traveled from Galveston on the invitation of Bishop John Mary Odin. Ten acres of land was purchased on the banks of the San Antonio River, and on November 7, 1851, the city's first school for "ladies of refinement" opened.

Most of the buildings on the old campus were constructed throughout the 1850s by architect Francois Giraud and contractor Jules Poinsard. The first academy building was finished in 1854 and used the "pise de terre" or rammed earth construction method. It is one of the few remaining examples of this type of construction left in the United States. Giraud was also responsible for the chapel and the unusual three-faced clock on the tower (at the time of construction, there was no development to the north, so no clock face was installed facing that direction).

After 120 years downtown, the academy was moved to its present location on Vance Jackson Road. In 1961 Mr. Link

Cowan of Oklahoma acquired the property on Augusta Street from the Catholic church. Cowan permitted a few nuns to remain living at the old campus until 1965, when he sold the property to the San Antonio Conservation Society. The Society plunged deep into debt to purchase several of the buildings, which were in an extreme state of disrepair and were becoming a haven for derelicts. On February 11, 1967, a fire destroyed the day students' building. It was all the firemen could do to save the remaining structures.

A five-year search for a new use for the academy ended in November of 1970, when the Southwest Craft Center leased the property for a dollar a year. In 1974 a $136,000 grant from the Economic Development Agency of the Commerce Department was secured and used for restoration. The craft center was finally able to purchase the property in 1975. The center is now home to galleries, classes, lectures, workshops, and artists in residence.

The Alamo Plaza Hotel - Formerly the Medical Arts Building

This neo-gothic building located on Alamo Plaza was originally the home to a small private hospital and a variety of medical offices. Built in 1926 and designed by Ralph Cameron, this thirteen-story building has long towered over its historic neighbor. Three generations of San Antonians have memories of the doctors who once occupied the building. The elaborate Gothic detail reflects the structure's earlier use. The faces that surround the first and second floor reflect patients suffering from different ailments. Medical crests also dot the facade. In 1978 the building was renovated into office space and renamed the Landmark Building.

In 1983 the Landmark was purchased by a group of investors who intended to turn it into a hotel. Since the inside of the building had already been gutted, little of the interior remained. About the only thing left inside from the old Medical Arts Building were the mail chute, the brass elevators, the original floor tiles, and a staircase. It took eighteen months and seventeen million dollars to turn former office space into a 177-room hotel. The hotel caters more to couples than to the business traveler. Each room features a whirlpool bath.

The name of the hotel has been a source of some controversy. Originally it was named the Emily Morgan Hotel for the famed Yellow Rose of Texas who tipped off Sam Houston that Santa Anna was planning an attack on San Jacinto. Some say Emily Morgan was a traitor and a prostitute. Others objected to the naming of a penthouse suite after Santa Anna. While some find it ironic, others found it offensive that the general who soundly defeated the defenders of the Alamo should have a suite named in his honor—especially when it overlooks the cradle of Texas liberty, the Alamo itself.

In the early '90s the hotel was renamed the Alamo Plaza Hotel.

Terrell Castle Bed and Breakfast - Formerly Lambermont

Located at 950 E. Grayson across from Ft. Sam Houston sits San Antonio's only castle. The castle was built by Edward Holland Terrell, who served as ambassador to Belgium from 1889 to 1893. Upon returning to San Antonio in 1894, Terrell commissioned architect Alfred Giles to build a home for his bride. He wanted it to resemble a castle of Europe that he admired.

The palatial home had twenty-six rooms and was complete with library, music room, solarium, wine cellar, and nine fireplaces. A room on the fourth floor has windows facing north, south, east, and west for a complete view of the city. The regal home was dubbed Lambermont after a business associate of the ambassador.

The family lived there until Terrell's death in 1908. Reportedly, Mrs. Terrell spent the rest of her life in Paris. Afterwards the home passed through the hands of many different owners. As the neighborhood decayed, the castle suffered the ultimate embarrassment, when it was divided into eight apartments in the midseventies. In 1986

Lambermont was restored by Katherine Poulis and Nancy Jane Haley, who opened up the castle as a bed and breakfast inn.

The mother/daughter pair became admirers of such inns after a trip out West, when they had the opportunity to stay at one in Provo, Utah. When they returned to San Antonio, they stopped one day to inspect the large home in their neighborhood that was up for sale. At the time, the building had no electricity, and they had to view the rooms with flashlights. When they were informed of the number of bedroom and bathrooms the castle had, they immediately thought about making it into a bed and breakfast inn.

Kathcrine Poulis was unaware of the history of the castle until after it was purchased. She believes that most San Antonians do not realize that a castle is within the city's limits. Most of her reputation comes from out-of-town visitors who have read about the castle in one of the many national publications which have featured the inn.

The Guenther House Restaurant - Formerly the private Guenther Residence

Built in 1860 by Carl Guenther, founder of the Pioneer Flour Mills, this private home has been transformed into a restaurant, museum, and gift shop. The building housed its last residents in 1948. After that, it had been used for storage. The dwelling sits on the edge of the King William District at the grounds of the Pioneer Flour Mill. It took fourteen months to refurbish the home before its grand reopening on March 22, 1988. Many of the furnishings in the restaurant, including the crystal chandelier, are family-owned pieces that originally were used in the former residence.

Artes Graficas Building, the Palace Livery Stable - now Law Offices

This building was constructed in 1910. The original painted sign for the Palace Livery Stable can still be seen faintly on the outside of this old building on Cameron Street.

It has served as everything from stables and a blacksmith shop to a fireworks company and a publishing company. It was renovated in 1980 and is now used as law offices.

Archival Storage Facility -
Formerly the Bexar County Jail

Across the street from the old Palace Livery Stable stands the old Bexar County Jail on 120 Cameron Street. The building was designed in 1862 by Alfred Giles and was completed in 1879 as a two-story structure. Additional floors were added in 1911 and 1926. In 1926 the jail also received a brick facade. In 1962 the jail moved to a new location across from the police station. The building was renovated in 1983 and became an archival storage facility.

The Metropolitan Health District Offices -
Formerly the Continental Hotel

This long office building on Commerce Street was built as the LaClede Hotel in 1898. It was later named the Continental Hotel. Legend has it that many Mexican revolutionaries stayed there in 1910. The hotel is now used for city offices.

The Rand Building -
Formerly the Wolff and Marx Department Store

This red brick structure on Houston Street was once home to Wolff and Marx, one of the city's premiere department stores. It was designed in 1913 by Sanguinet and Staats, Dallas architects famous for building "skyscrapers." The structure was once the downtown home of USAA Insurance. The building was set for demolition in 1981 but was saved when the building was purchased by the San Antonio Conservation Society, who sought out a developer to renovate it. Randstone Ventures bought the structure and converted it to office space.

The Argyle Club - Formerly the Argyle Hotel

This exclusive private club located in the heart of Alamo Heights benefits the Southwest Foundation for Research and Education. The building is an old ranch home that later became a hotel. It was built years before anything else in Alamo Heights. The name Argyle was given to the hotel by the two Scotsmen who operated the establishment in honor of their home county in Scotland.

The Aurora Apartments - Originally the Aurora Hotel

The dominating structure overlooking Crockett Park just off Main Street was once an exclusive hotel for the privileged. Built in 1930, it served as a San Antonio home to many of society's finest.

By the 1970s the Aurora fell on hard times. Its last tenant was KISS radio, the last of the underground rock radio stations. The building was without running water or elevator service (a major nuisance for a station located on the 8th floor). In the early 1980s the building was refurbished into apartments for the elderly.

Old Prospect Hill Baptist Church - Now Apartments for the Elderly

Many architects agree that this old church has been the city's most amazing restoration and conversion project. The building at 1601 Buena Vista was built in 1911 to house a large congregation. As the demographics of the neighborhood changed, church membership began to shrink. In 1965 they disbanded.

In 1980 the church was nearly destroyed by fire. Soon after, work began to rehabilitate the building into housing for the elderly. The exterior of the structure is virtually unchanged with the exception of a red dome that replaced the fire damaged original. The inside, though, has been totally remodeled, leaving few signs of its former heritage.

G. J. Sutton State Office Building -
Formerly the San Antonio Machine and Supply Company

This former factory near St Paul square was built in the 1880s with additions in 1904, 1906, and 1912. SAMSCO's glory days were in the early 20th century when there was a large market for their windmills and ranching supplies. The state of Texas purchased the eastside plant in 1975 and converted it to office space.

John H. Wood U.S. Courthouse -
Formerly the U.S. Pavilion for Hemisfair

This federal courthouse at Hemisfair Park was originally the Confluence Theatre for the 1968 World's Fair. The near-by Institute of Texan Cultures is another leftover from Hemisfair. It was formerly the Texas Pavilion.

Melodrama Playhouse - Originally Schultze Store

Located at the west entrance of Hemisfair Plaza, this is one of only a handful of structures that was spared the wrecking ball that decimated the neighborhood earmarked for the World's Fair. The structure features finely detailed cast iron work that was made locally and is one of the last Italiante-style commercial buildings left in the city.

Other structures in town that have been saved include the old Menger Soap Factory, which is now an office for the Soapworks Apartments downtown; the Mexican Consulate which at one time housed the Federal Reserve; and the Mexican American Unity Council, which makes its home in a 70-year-old elementary school in Prospect Hill.

Several majestic private homes have been saved from the wrecking ball and now serve wider purposes. The Koehler House, which once was the home of the Pearl Brewery heirs is now used by San Antonio College. The Junior League has its offices in the former home of Cladius King and the Conservation Society uses the former Anton Wulff home as its headquarters.

GONE, BUT NOT FORGOTTEN

Hot Wells Hotel

As the city of San Antonio moves into its third century, it is rapidly becoming dependent on a tourist-based economy. But a glance back into the history of the city shows that San Antonio was once before a tourist destination for the well-heeled traveler. Supplied with hot mineral water from the Edwards Aquifer, the San Antonio area sprouted many resorts in the early part of the century, not unlike those of Mineral Wells, Texas; Hot Springs, Arkansas; or Saratoga Springs, New York.

The Hot Wells Hotel.

The industry began with a modest discovery in 1892, when an artesian well containing sulfurized water was discovered by the board of directors at the Southwestern Lunatic Asylum (now known as the San Antonio State Hospital). The water was found unfit to drink, but the board of directors (which included Sam Maverick and Daniel

Oppenheimer) realized the significance of their discovery. To defray the cost of an alternate water source, the asylum leased the water rights for $75 to Charles Scheuermeyer, who was the first to realize the medicinal possibilities of the sulfurized springs. From 1892 to 1983 Scheuermeyer's Southwestern Park and Hot Sulphur Natatorium were operated near the present site of the Hot Wells Hotel. Scheuermeyer advertised that the waters were a cure for rheumatism, kidney, liver and skin diseases, and blood poisoning.

On May 5, 1893, McClellan Shacklett outbid Charles Scheuermeyer for the rights to the spring for ten years. Under the terms of the lease, Shacklett was obligated to pay $500 a year and build a first-class bathhouse and hotel. A ten-acre pecan grove on the banks of the San Antonio River was purchased as a site for a premiere facility. Plans were also made to extend the city's streetcar line out to the site. In less than a year, the pecan grove was transformed into a landscaped park with carriage trails. The newly constructed bathhouse featured private bathing and a public pool. The new facility was known as Natural Hot Spring Wells or Hot Sulphur Baths.

In the late 1800s and early 1900s, mineral baths such as the ones in San Antonio became destinations for society's elite. The baths were thought to offer a certain therapeutic effect which provided cures for all sorts of ailments. Shacklett's resort boasted that bathing and drinking the sulphur water would relieve diseases of the liver, kidneys, stomach, and bowels. It would cure skin diseases such as eczema, erysipelas, blotches, boils, carbuncles, scaldhead, herpes, hair loss, nettlerash, and old chronic sores that had resisted healing. It also aided people suffering from rheumatic gout or paralysis, malaria, chronic diarrhea, weak eyes, weak backs, or tapeworms.

Resorts such as Hot Sulphur Wells also offered social activities, such as formal balls, dances, and dinners. A small menagerie was also an attraction at the resort. A variety of exotic animals, along with a black bear sent by Judge Roy

Bean, were featured at the zoo. With trolley cars running out to the hotel every twenty minutes, the resort became a popular destination for local residents, who used the pool as a way to escape the stifling summer heat of San Antonio.

Tragedy struck the resort in the early morning hours of December 23, 1894, when flames swept through the bathhouse. Shacklett personally rescued six patrons who were staying in the guest rooms. The entire structure was totally destroyed in less than an hour. Shacklett decided to rebuild on a grander scale, but he lost his lease on the "crazy waters" to a group of investors who convinced the city that Shacklett had been unfaithful to the terms of the lease. The new investors secured a new twenty-five-year lease because they argued the temporary natatorium that was built after the fire was substandard and violated the previous lease agreement.

In 1900 a new era began for the springs as the Texas Hot Sulphur Water Sanitarium Company opened for business with Otto Koelhler as president. The new company purchased the land with intent to build a new facility. By September three new swimming pools were built—one for each gender and one for families. A third tract of land was bought in 1901, and a hotel was completed that year.

The hotel was a three-story brick building with three wings that opened up into a courtyard. In contained eighty first-class rooms that provided modern conveniences such as hot and cold water, steam heat, telephones to the office, electric and gas lights, and fine furnishings. Masseurs and private baths were available, as were solid porcelain tubs plus steam, Turkish, Russian, and Roman baths. The swimming pools were lined with white enamel bricks (a smart move considering San Antonio's lime problem). Advertisements for the spa were placed in newspapers as far away as New York and Chicago, comparing the spa to the best in the world.

Other attractions soon followed. An ostrich farm relocated from San Pedro Springs Park about that time. Ladies from the city and those staying at the resort would travel to the farm for feathers, which were quite the fashion statement of the period. A bowling club featuring both nine-pin and ten-pin lanes opened up in 1902, and in 1906 the Cincinnati Reds held spring training there. The International Fair and Exhibition held at nearby Riverside Park also attracted guests until the fair closed in 1904.

The resort continued to grow. In 1906 it was reported that approximately 2000 guests had to be turned away. Late the next year, work began on an addition that would add ninety rooms, making it one of the largest hotels in the Southwest. New landscaping and a palm garden were included in the plans. A new streetcar line brought visitors from downtown for a mere nickel.

Transportation, in the form of the railroad, propelled the Hot Sulphur Wells Resort to a new level when E. H. Harriman, a railroad tycoon, visited in 1909. Harriman had a spur built that connected the hotel to the main tracks of his San Antonio & Aransas Pass Railroad. Harriman was able to take his private rail car right to the resort grounds. Harriman visited the Wells to improve his poor health. The rail tycoon arrived in February of 1909 and left when his health improved, which he attributed to the "crazy waters." A 1910 promotional book for the facility includes a letter from Harriman dated March 1, 1910, that endorses the facility. However, Harriman died in September of 1909.

With the addition of the rail spur, the resort enjoyed even more success. New attractions included tennis, horseback riding, and gambling parlors. A garage was now provided for patrons with automobiles. The Star Film Company established field offices at the resort in 1911. That company, along with other filmmakers, used the area around the hotel for filming many westerns. Sarah Bernhardt arrived at the hotel in her private rail car for an extended stay with the film company, and Cecil B. deMille visited the company and stayed at the resort in the early days of the film business.

Many smaller hotels sprang up around the hotel for those who wished to visit the sulphur baths but needed more economical accommodations. The nearby ostrich farm staged weekly races at the resort for the enjoyment of the many gamblers who frequented the resort. The ostrich farm remained until 1920, when it became a victim of changing fashion. As the ostrich feather went out of style, so went the farm. The birds were donated to Brackenridge Zoo. The hotel continued to attract a high-class clientele, however. Visitors included Rudolph Valentino, Douglas Fairbanks, Will Rogers, Hoot Gibson, Tom Mix, Teddy Roosevelt, Mrs. J. P. Morgan, and Portfirio Diaz, many of whom traveled via their private rail cars.

The hotel continued to flourish until 1917. The effect of World War I and prohibition had a profound effect on the resort. When the elite clientele stopped coming, the management tried to lure more locals in with a mix of formal dinners and orchestra performances. The hotel continued to falter, and during World War I, the resort was used to house officers and their families from Brooks Field.

The Hot Wells Hotel: Part II

In 1923 the Hot Wells Hotel was purchased by Christian Scientists and converted into the El Dorado School. The parochial school used the hotel as a dormitory and the bathhouse for its classrooms. On January 17, 1925, the old hotel building caught fire, leaving only the outer bricks intact. The fire department pumped water from the river and was able to save the bathhouse. The building burned in about thirty minutes due to poor water pressure. About 10,000 San Antonians watched as the once majestic hotel was engulfed in flames.

In 1927 the old resort was converted into the Hot Wells Tourist Court. Ownership changed often; W. W. McAllister was once an owner. Cabins were built to house guests who were allowed to use the pool in the bathhouse. From 1930 to 1933 a sanitarium operated on the land along with the tourist court.

McAllister sold the property to Mrs. Cleo S. Jones in 1942. She and her husband Ralph Jones converted the twenty-one acres into a trailer park and motel. In 1944 the Joneses

converted the bathhouse into the Flame Room, a neighborhood bar and grill. Mr. Jones inherited the property in 1961
after his wife's death. He and his second wife Hattie continued to allow swimmers in the bathhouse for one dollar.
By the midseventies, most of the cabins were vacant, and
only a few permanent residents lived in the trailer park.

In 1977 the Joneses, in their eighties, finally closed the
Flame Room and agreed to sell the property to anybody
willing to refurbish the hotel. The contents of the old hotel
were auctioned off in August of 1977. In December of 1979
Kathryn Scheer purchased the property with hopes of restor-
ing the resort.

During the next eleven years, thousands of dollars were
spent on studies to determine a future use for the hotel.
Various plans called for a holistic health center, a conference
center, a resort, and a stop along the Mission Parkway. With
restoration plans nearing completion, tragedy struck once
again.

On the night of June 27, 1988, flames ravaged the old
bathhouse. The caretaker stated that lightning struck the
steeple about 6:30, but it was an hour before flames were
visible. Old wooden beams and extremely dry wood fed the
vicious flames for two hours. Since the building had been
condemned, there was no insurance. The building was on
the National Register of Historic Places, and the loss to the
city could not be put in terms of a dollar value. After the fire,
the owner stated that the outer brick wall was still intact, so
there might still be a chance of renovation.

The Bluebonnet Hotel and the Mysterious Robert Johnson

On the corner of St. Mary's Street and Martin is a small privately owned park with a sign that reads "Use at Your Own Risk." At one time, the Bluebonnet Hotel sat on this corner. It was torn down in 1988 by the M Bank Corporation, which had plans to tear down the rest of the block and build an office tower. With the failure of M Bank, those plans are now questionable.

The Bluebonnet was a favorite of conservationists who tried to save it with thoughts of converting it into apartments. Because of the design of the building, any large-scale remodeling effort would have been practically impossible. The hotel closed its doors in February 1985.

The hotel made its place in history in 1936 when legendary blues guitarist Robert Johnson recorded there. Johnson, dubbed the "King of the Delta Blues," lived a life that was shrouded in mystery. Some sources say he was born in Hazelhurst, Mississippi; others say Robinsville, Mississippi. Some believe he was about thirty years old when he came to San Antonio to record; others, including his producer Don Law, remember him being only seventeen or eighteen. Photographs of him are as rare as good information. However, few people disagree on the talent that Robert Johnson possessed. Johnson was a new and different kind of bluesman, who could make his guitar scream to match his powerful voice.

Johnson came to San Antonio after meeting with American Recording Company talent scout Ernie Oertle. Oertle cut a deal and sent the guitarist to the Alamo City to record for Vocalion Records, a subsidiary of ARC. Though he did not stay at the Bluebonnet Hotel (he stayed at a segregated hotel), Johnson did record there, in the studios of

KONO radio. On November 23, 1936, he recorded eight songs, including "Dust My Broom," which would later become a hit for Elmore James.

The next day Johnson disappeared. The country boy from Mississippi was obviously overwhelmed by the entertainment options a city the size of San Antonio offered. Nobody is quite sure what kind of trouble he got into, but his producer Don Law had to make a trip down to the police department where Johnson was being held on a vagrancy charge. On November 26 he resumed recording, laying down the tune "32-20 Blues." On the next day he put seven more songs to tape, including "Crossroads Blues," a song that Eric Clapton and Cream would later turn into a platinum record which would inspire the movie *Crossroads*.

Because of the limited distribution of the records (the songs were only released in the South and usually only bought by black music customers), Johnson's vinyl offerings became instant collectors' items. Only one song, "Terraplane Blues," ever really sold well to the general public.

In 1938 John Hammond was planning his "Spiritual Swing" concert for Carnegie Hall. Hammond has become a legend in the music business for producing such greats as Bessie Smith, Benny Goodman, and Stevie Ray Vaughan. Hammond sought help from ARC producer Don Law in locating Johnson. Law discovered that Johnson had been poisoned to death a few days earlier by a jealous girlfriend.

A brilliant talent, and possibly a successful career, was tragically cut short. Details about the bluesman's life remain sketchy, but the Bluebonnet Hotel sessions have become legendary and have assured Johnson a place in music history.

Brock's Books

A landmark of downtown San Antonio, Brock's Books, located at 312 E. Commerce, closed its doors one final time in January, 1987. Norman Brock, Sr., or "Poor Broke Brock" as he was sometimes known, was 78 years old, and running his bookstore finally came in second to retirement.

In March of 1986 Brock Sr. decided it was time to take life easy. The bookstore was turned over to his son, Norman Brock, Jr. The store was his father's life, but Brock Jr. had a life of his own. He worked as an engineer, and he was raising a family near Houston. Running a bookstore that wasn't turning a profit in an area of San Antonio that isn't kind to merchants was a challenge that Brock Jr. decided not to take. After all, he was an engineer—not a bookseller.

Brock Jr. decided to sell the store. He offered over a million books and the largest collection of National Geographics in the world, all for a price of $35,000. Two parties were interested in Brock's merchandise. One was a bookseller from Houston, and the other was from Portland, Oregon. Both realized that this was quite a bargain, but they both ended up turning down the offer because the collection was simply too large. To move the books out of the basement alone would take eleven moving vans.

So, Brock Jr. began to dispose of the collection section by section. Over 8000 pieces of Texana were donated to the Daughters of the Alamo, who gladly accepted the gift. One of Brock's employees, Jeanne Stone, bought a portion of the collection to start her own used book store. The National Geographics were put on sale at $10 for a thousand. Everything in the famous basement was being sold for a mere 50 cents.

The once-crowded aisles were now beginning to widen. The walls and shelves, which once were crowded with countless volumes, began to show gaps and spaces. But it takes a long time to sell one million books, even at ridiculously low prices. So Brock Jr. began giving them away. Each hour the employees took more books to the front of the store for passerbys to browse through and walk away with a five-finger discount. Brock Jr. figured that he gave away over two hundred thousand books. The no-cost books moved so fast that every two hours a totally new selection of books was being offered for free.

While sorting through the massive inventory, the younger Brock found some true gems. Included were a letter written by Sam Houston, photographs of Santa Anna's army taken in 1841, one of the original charters for the city of San Antonio, and original newspapers announcing the deaths of George Washington and Abraham Lincoln. Most of these items were saved for his father, Brock Sr.

The dispersement of the collection is something the elder Brock did not witness. It took the better part of a lifetime to collect it and less than a year to sell it.

The store was important to more people than just the Brocks. It was also a major part of Johnnie Rink's life. He had worked at Brock's for twenty years, and he saw downtown become a difficult territory for a merchant. "It is hard," said Rink, "for the store to make a profit, when most San Antonians do not want to drive downtown and pay three dollars to park just to buy four dollars' worth of books."

In early February of 1987, the last books were sold, along with the furniture and the fixtures. Everything was either sold or given away; nothing was thrown away. When the last pages in the last book left the store, Norman Brock, Jr., turned out the lights of Brock's Books. Forever.

Department Stores

For the first half of this century, every major American city had a variety of locally owned department stores. Texas was no different. Houston had Foley's; Dallas had Neiman-Marcus; Fort Worth had Monnings. San Antonio had three major department stores. Two eventually evolved to become regional chains. By 1990 all three had vanished, but they left an impact on the city that will be felt for years.

Wolff & Marx

Started in 1877, by Albert A. Wolff and Daniel Marx, in a small adobe house located on West Commerce Street, Wolff & Marx later became known as the city's skyscraper department store. In 1913 the store moved into a new eight-story structure at 210 W. Houston. The retail outlet dwarfed its neighbors. Eight stories was a big deal in 1913.

Ironically, Wolff & Marx's demise was due to the fact that it was too successful. It was purchased by Joske's, in 1965, who coveted their branch in North Star Mall. Joske's announced plans to close the downtown branch because it became obsolete (meaning the building could not accommodate escalators). For a while, Wolff & Marx and Joske's operated as a joint operation, but eventually the North Star branch became Joske's, and Wolff & Marx disappeared forever.

Joske's

The San Antonio retail legend started modestly in 1873, by Julius Joske in a one-room adobe building on Austin Street. An earlier effort to start a dry goods store failed, but on the second venture he had the help of his sons Siegfried, Albert, and Alexander. In 1875 a new store opened on Alamo

Plaza with a new name, Joske Brothers. The store moved again to its historic spot on Commerce and Alamo in 1888.

The new two-story outlet known as the "Big Store" was an immediate hit. In 1903 two more stories were added, as well as elevators. The first escalators in San Antonio were added in 1935—the same year Joske's became the first air conditioned department store in Texas.

The store was famous for "The Big Sign" that hovered over Alamo Plaza for many years. Many remember the sign being atop the Joske's, but actually it was atop the adjacent Conroy Building. The fifty by five foot sign, famous for its giant cowboy roping a steer, was used to advertise a variety of businesses until Joske's bought the building and began using the sign exclusively.

Joske's eventually tore down the neighboring building, expanding in 1939 and 1953, until it took up virtually the whole block. One neighbor decided not to sell, so the department store just built around them. For years the German Catholic Church that was surrounded on three sides by the new additions was known simply as St. Joske's. The new store was dubbed the largest store in the largest state (after Alaska was admitted to the Union it became known as the grandest store in the grandest state). The big sign that was supposed to be reerected atop the new store never returned. Structural problems would not permit the sign to be placed atop the newly remodeled store. In 1942 the sign was donated to a wartime scrap metal drive.

The greatest time to visit the downtown store was during Christmas. It was then that the store set up its elaborate Fantasyland that entertained generations of the city's youngsters. Opening in 1960, it attracted over one million visitors in its first five years. Talking Bears, the Magic Train, The Church of Every Faith, Santa's Castle, and the Fantasyland Town Square were featured. Outside, a giant Santa adorned the roof (during Easter, Peter Rabbit sat on the roof).

Joske's opened its first branch in 1957, at the Las Palmas Shopping Center (an H.E.B. now occupies the site). Eventually, seven Joske's stores stretched across Texas. In 1987 the downtown store closed for remodeling. Rivercenter Mall was being built on the old parking lot, and they were preparing the store to be one of the anchor tenants. Unfortunately, Joske's never reopened. The Dillard department store chain bought out the seven outlets and announced plans to convert them into Dillard stores. Despite much outcry and pleading by conservationists, the Joske's name became history. The large letters on the corners of the building were removed and replaced with a Rivercenter sign. The biggest store in the biggest state became nothing more than a memory.

The funeral procession of Alexander Joske on July 10, 1925, as it passes by his store.

Frost Brothers

Frost Brothers department stores originated in 1917, by Jonas and William Frost, when the two dry goods merchants bought a dress store at 217 Houston. This art deco outlet catered to San Antonio's upper crust for many years. In 1949 the store doubled in size when it expanded straight through to Travis Street. To travel from the Men's Department on Travis Street to the Women's Department on Houston Street, patrons had to cross through an alley. Frost Brothers eventually had locations in North Star Mall, Crossroads Mall, and nine other locations throughout the state.

The downtown store closed in 1987 for remodeling. The department store vowed to reopen when construction on Houston Street was finished and when the Majestic remodeling was complete. Many feared that the historic downtown branch would never open again.

It never would. In 1989 Frost Brothers announced it was going out of business. On June 29 the North Star Mall store closed, leaving San Antonio without a homegrown department store.

The Grand Opera House

Located across from the Alamo, the Grand Opera House was once the site of the city's premier social events. Opening in 1886, the performing arts hall sat 1500 patrons in solid oak chairs with mohair upholstery. Designed by J. P. McElpatric and Son of St. Louis, the Grand was considered one of the finest in the country. Its opening night featured Emma Abbott and Lucretia Borgia, two top performers of the time.

The opera house had most of its success during its first two years. When motion pictures came in vogue, the Grand began showing the new medium. Shortly after World War I, the Grand Opera House closed. The building was modified and became the H. L. Green variety store. Green's closed in the 1980s and the building is now the home of a wax museum and a Ripley's Believe It or Not showcase.

The Grand Opera House.

The Vance House

This colonial mansion was built by James Vance in 1859 on 210 East Nueva. Nance, from Stebaune, Ireland, built the home for his bride. The home was one of San Antonio's finest, built with lumber and wrought iron brought from New Orleans. Running water was a feature of this stately home; a water tank affixed to the roof made this one of the first buildings to offer such a luxury. The mansion was host to many dignitaries, including Robert E. Lee. In the 1930s the Vance House was chosen by the Department of the Interiors's Historic Building Survey as an outstanding architectural example.

The Vance House passed through various owners; at one time, it was home to Texas State Employment Service. The stately mansion was torn down in the early 1950s and was replaced with the new Federal Reserve Bank. A plaque now rests at the site of the home.

Playland Park

Two generations of San Antonians have fond memories of a small amusement park known simply as Playland Park. The fifteen-acre park was opened in 1941 by Jimmy Johnson, a former Army soldier, who had the idea for the park when he was stationed at Fort Sam and saw the need for a place where folks could gather for good clean fun.

Johnson first opened an amusement center on the polo field at Brackenridge Park. In 1941 he moved to a new home at the corner of North Alamo and Broadway, which was one of the main thoroughfares into the city and quite a busy intersection. Johnson personally designed many of the rides and attractions at Playland Park. One of his favorites was something called, "What Every Man Knows About Women."

Playland Park in its heyday. Note the admission price.

When a park goer deposited ten cents, he would get to peek inside and see nothing, and Johnson would enjoy a private laugh.

Some of the more popular rides included the Rocket Roller Coaster, the Transylvania Trolley, the Zoomer, and a 1917 carousel. However, Playland Park was more than rides. Johnson added other attractions, too, such as the Pleasant Valley Chapel, which provided park goers with a place for meditation. The Paper Eating Clowns with the Vacuum Mouths were a popular feature at the park with young kids, who could not wait to throw away their soda cups and their hot dog wrappers. Mother Goose Land, the miniature Mount Rushmore, and the Liberty Bell Replica were just some of the special touches that Johnson added to make Playland Park a one-of-a-kind place.

In September of 1980, the day after Labor Day, Johnson closed the doors forever. He claimed to have lost money for the last ten years, citing taxes and high utility rates for the park's demise. Johnson was also critical of the city government for supporting a midway on Hemisfair Plaza with his tax dollars.

The growth of such places as Astroworld and Six Flags Over Texas surely did not help his business. With an advanced highway system, both places were easily accessible by the family car. At the time of Playland Park's closing, it cost ten dollars to get into Astroworld. It took only twenty-five cents to get into Playland

When Jimmy Johnson closed Playland, he said, "It's like losing a child." Many of the attractions were bought by other amusement parks. The roller coaster was moved to Pennsylvania, and the chapel was moved to the north side and converted into an Anglican Catholic church. In later years the old proprietor would charge five dollars to curiosity seekers who wanted to visit the park. Johnson often said, "When you retire, you die." The man who brought so many San Antonians thirty-nine years of good clean fun died three years later.

Alamo Downs

Now that pari-mutuel gambling is again legal in Texas, many groups have come forward with intentions of building a local track. If a track is built in San Antonio, it will not be the city's first. Over fifty years ago, San Antonio was a hotbed for horse racing. Located at the edge of town, where Culebra and 410 now meet, Alamo Downs drew many top jockeys from Chicago and the East during its sixty-day winter season.

Alamo Downs in 1937

Alamo Downs, built by Raymond Russell, opened on April 2, 1934, with an overflow crowd of 12,000. Governor Ma Ferguson was just one of the dignitaries on hand. Throughout the Depression, the track averaged a crowd of over 5,000 patrons. Most caught the bus at the corner of Travis and St. Mary's, which took them to the track on the edge of town. Many came to escape the Depression, and only a small number gambled. At the time, the bookies were often suspected of conducting unfair practices, and more than once the day ended with a confrontation between angry track goers and bookmakers.

In 1937 then-governor Jimmy Allred, with backing from the Baptist church, called a special session of the legislature, and legal pari-mutuel betting was repealed. Between 1937 and 1987 thirteen attempts to legalize gambling were brought to the legislature, and all were defeated. When pari-mutuel betting finally did become legal in 1987, Alamo Downs was long gone. The site eventually became a home to a salvage yard. Ten years after its closing, a fire swept through the grandstand, destroying most of the facility. For many years the Alamo Downs sign could still be seen near Culebra Road, and cows could be seen grazing on the infield near the old burnt out grandstand.

Today the site of Alamo Downs is now occupied by a business park. What once was the edge of town is now sandwiched between Holmes High School and Northwest Stadium, and it is across the highway from Ingram Park Mall. The new facility in the racetrack's place is aptly called Alamo Downs Business Park.

Peacock Military Academy

Located near Woodlawn Lake for seventy-nine years, this military school was started in 1894 by Professor Wesley Peacock, who moved to San Antonio to start a boarding school known as the Peacock School for Boys. San Antonio was an ideal site for a boarding school for boys, due to its proximity to Fort Sam Houston, one of the nation's largest military posts. The city was also a growing metropolis, with an excellent economic base and rail transportation. Military training began in 1900, the same year a new 2 ½-story building was erected on the grounds near West End Lake (as Woodlawn Lake was called back then).

In 1904 the school was chartered by the state of Texas and was one of the first three institutions recognized by the U.S. government. Enrollment peaked during the first World War, when Army officers readied young men for military service. From 1920 to 1926 the school was used by the Veterans' Bureau as a vocational training facility for ex-servicemen. In 1926 the school officially became Peacock Military Academy and was being run by Wesley Peacock's sons, Wesley Jr. and Donald Peacock. The Academy became widely known for its excellent drill teams, who won much recognition for their percussion, and for a football team that was once coached by a young Army lieutenant named Dwight Eisenhower.

In 1973 the school closed its doors for good. The facility, consisting of fifteen buildings and fifteen acres, was transferred to the Salvation Army.

Hipp's Bubble Room

This tiny bar, formerly located at 1411 N. McCollough, was torn down in 1980 for that great local institution . . . a parking lot. Once the favorite hangout for downtown workers, businessmen, lawyers, and anybody else who didn't mind the cramped surroundings, the bar was owned and operated by L. D. Hipp. Its name was derived from the hundreds of bubbling Christmas lights that decorated the premises.

The Christmas lights were a year-round attraction, as was the always present Christmas tree, the rubber balls hanging from the ceiling, the crushed tin foil decorations, and the toy train known as the H.I.P. & P. Railroad. Hipp's Bubble Room gained its charm from its excessive tackiness.

The bar measured only sixty feet by sixty-five feet and was housed in a former carriage house. It existed for over thirty years and became the favorite San Antonio hangout for Peter Ustinov and Jonathon Winters. Winters was such a big fan, that he once ordered 144 shypoke eggs (Hipp's special appetizer) for a Hollywood party. Hipp had his famous creation sent by air freight in time to make the party.

Throughout the 1950s, Hipp's was the largest retailer of Pearl Beer. However, Hipp switched to Lone Star when the Pearl Distributor refused to sell him green beer for St. Patrick's Day. Hipp originated the famous "Gimmedraw" (an inexpensive draught beer), and he often lent the Conservation Society his beer license during Fiesta.

The good times ended at Hipp's in 1980. The landlord, Metropolitan Professional Buildings Inc., claimed the building was an eyesore and wanted Hipp's gone. They quadrupled the rent and got a city code enforcer to limit the number of patron's to thirty-one. Hipp claimed that the landlord made no improvements to the alleged eyesore, and that it was impossible for him to survive with only thirty-one people allowed in the bar at a time. During Fiesta Week 1980, he was served his eviction notice. The Bubble Room closed for good on May 24, 1980, and was razed on June 17. It was replaced by four rarely used parking spaces.

Across the street is Little Hipp's, a hamburger joint started by Hipp's son. The old gas station/now restaurant received many of the decorations that once adorned the Bubble Room. As for the expanded parking lot, the four spaces remain empty most of the time.

The 12th Hole

The 19th hole is usually the traditional stopping place for golfers. After a full day of play, linksters will retire to the 19th hole for a few cool ones and perhaps a snack or two. Ask any old-timer about the 12th hole at Brackenridge Golf Course, and he will tell you about the best burgers and the coldest beer this side of Augusta.

For many years, just beyond the 12th green at Brack was a small privately owned snack bar called the 12th Hole, that sold whatever a golfer required, as long as it could be cooked on a grill or kept in a cooler. It was the perfect way to beat the heat. Often a golfing party would play twelve holes, then stop and refresh themselves before finishing the final six holes.

When McAllister Freeway was built, it cut severely into the Brackenridge course. Consequently, the course had to be reshaped, making it much smaller than the original version. The 12th hole was the biggest casualty. The green was on the other side of the freeway, leaving it and the restaurant completely cut off from the course.

The 12th Hole restaurant tried to make it on its own for years after, but it was difficult to reach. It passed through different owners and finally closed in 1985. The building and the green still exist—just take Terry Court off North St. Mary's, near the Ashby/St. Mary's intersection.

Whopper Burger

This local hamburger fast food chain set the standard for San Antonians for decades. There was not a neighborhood in San Antonio that did not feature a Whopper Burger. Some came for the crinkle fries, others stopped for the orange freeze, and still others enjoyed the orange and white decor. It sometimes seemed that no two Whopper Burger buildings were the same. Some were modern, with slick clean lines, like the one on Wurzbach and I-10. Others were a celebration of neon, as was the restaurant on San Pedro, just south of North Star Mall. (This particular Whopper Burger was featured in the movie *Johnny Be Good*.) Some featured the old and outdated, robust "Whopper Boy" logo.

Because the local chain held the rights to the term "Whopper," Burger King was unable to open restaurants in San Antonio. In 1986 the Pillsbury Company (which owned the national chain) bought out Whopper Burger. Soon, the home of the original whopper was gone.

Some of the locations closed down, others became used car lots, and some were transformed into Burger Kings. Many simply changed names and very little else. Today, you may stop at a Murf's Better Burger or a Burger Boy, but, deep down, you're stopping at San Antonio's favorite hamburger stand, Whopper Burger.

SECTION V

THE SPORTS PAGE

Baseball in the Alamo City

Organized baseball started in San Antonio over 100 years ago with the formation of the Texas League of Professional Baseball Clubs. Unfortunately, the San Antonio team only started the season, dropping out in the middle of the year. The team reentered the league in 1892, but the league folded this time. The fledging baseball team finally got rolling in 1895 and brought home its first championship in 1897. From 1903 till 1906, San Antonio, along with Houston, Galveston, Austin, and a host of other teams, formed the South Texas League of which San Antonio was the champion in 1903. The San Antonio Bronchos won their first Texas League Championship in 1908, one year after reentering the league.

San Antonio was a member of the league for over 50 years, winning championships in 1933, 1950, 1961, 1963, and 1964. In 1964 the San Antonio Bullets were disbanded, and the city was left without a team for three years. The team was owned by Judge Roy Hofheinz, who also owned the National League's Houston Colt .45s (later to be known as the Houston Astros). Hofheinz believed that the Bullets were competition for the Astros and pulled the plug on the team and padlocked the stadium. The city was without a team until 1968 when the Chicago Cubs placed a farm team here.

San Antonio teams have won very few championships considering the amount of time spent in the league; however, add to their seven titles the 1950 Dixie Series and the 1961 Pan American Series Championship. In 1920 the winner of the Texas League started a year-end series with the winner of the Southern Association. The Missions lost to the New Orleans Pelicans. The 1950 series saw the Missions beat the Nashville Vols. The Dixie Series was replaced by the Pan American Series in which the Texas League Champions played the winners of the Mexican League. The Missions won the last series in 1961 when they beat Vera Cruz. These postseason series were a victim of televised major league baseball. In 1950 league attendance dropped 300,000 from the previous season. The Dixie Series and the Pan American Series were unable to compete with the World Series.

The Missions did enjoy radio broadcasts of their games starting in 1929 on KTAP. Earl Wilson was the first play by play man followed by popular Sam Goldfarb, known by the unusual nickname "Boliver Dugag," on KABC radio, owned and operated by the Alamo Broadcasting Corporation.

The San Antonio team has had a variety of nicknames including the Shamrocks, Indians, Bears, Missionaries, Bronchos, Brewers, Bullets (the Bullets supplied the major league Colt .45s), Dodgers (an L.A. Dodger farm club), and the Missions. "The Missions" by far has been the most popular nickname, in use for the majority of the team's existence. In 1988 the San Antonio Dodgers were rechristened the Missions, much to the delight of many old-time fans.

Many great major leaguers played for San Antonio, including Joe Morgan, Babe Herman, Brooks Robinson, Steve Sax, Ramon Martinez, and Fernando Valenzuela. Valenzuela led the S.A. Dodgers to the Texas League Western Division Title in 1980 and was scheduled to pitch the opening game of the Texas League Championship when he got called up to the parent Los Angeles Dodgers for a crucial series with the Houston Astros. While the local team lost three straight to the Arkansas Travelers, Valenzuela sat on the bench for the major league Dodgers.

From 1933 until the 1950s, the Missions were a farm team of the St. Louis Browns and later the Baltimore Orioles. San Antonio has also farmed out players to the Houston Colt .45s, the Chicago Cubs, and the Los Angeles Dodgers. Many major league teams also trained here during the twenties and thirties. Native Texan Rogers Hornsby brought his great Cardinals in the spring, including the 1926 World Champions. Hornsby felt the San Antonio spring climate best matched the St. Louis summer climate, not to mention the fact that he enjoyed the hot springs at Terrell Wells. Babe Ruth and the Yankees made a stop in San Antonio on March 31, 1931. The Brooklyn Dodgers also barnstormed through the city. Both teams had their pictures taken by noted San Antonio photographer E. O. Goldbeck during their stops.

Babe Ruth cracking a home run at League Park in the first inning on the way to a 14-4 rout of the San Antonio Indians, March 31, 1930.

Babe Ruth outside the Menger Hotel.

The Stadiums

San Antonio's baseball clubs have practiced their trade in a variety of shops. Currently, the San Antonio Missions play at V. J. Keefe Field on the campus of St. Mary's University. The stadium allows the fans to be very close to the playing field, and every seat has an excellent line of sight. From the seats above first base, you can see the downtown skyline. Most Mission fans agree that V. J. Keefe Field is a great place to watch a game. Unfortunately, the park only holds 4000, which is the smallest in the league. The team has played there since 1968.

Mission Stadium was perhaps the finest minor league facility in the country. It was built in 1947 by the St. Louis Browns at a cost of $750,000. The stadium was located off Mission Road on the south side and sat 9500 fans. Texas League players agreed that the stadium was truly a first-class facility. The field was always kept in fine shape and the lighting was excellent (which can be rare in minor league parks). The Baltimore Orioles (formerly the St. Louis Browns) passed control of the stadium to the Houston Colt .45s and Judge Roy Hofheinz in 1962. The San Antonio Bullets played there until 1965 when Hofheinz pulled the team out of the city and padlocked the stadium. The judge refused offers for the facility from many native San Antonians, and eventually it fell into disrepair. The ballpark sat vacant until 1973 when it was sold to a Houston developer who tore it down in 1974. It is now the site of the city's juvenile delinquent facility. Fans who attended games there felt a great loss at its destruction.

Another stadium in San Antonio was Tech Field located at North Flores and Evergreen, now site of the VIA bus garages. The field held only 2000 and was really set up to be only a high school field for the Technical High School. But the field was called into service in the middle of the 1933 season when League Park burned down.

League Park, also known as Bear Field or Bear Park, was located on Josephine Street about 100 yards from Boehler's Beer Garden (now the Liberty Bar). The field was the site of the St. Louis Cardinals' spring training, the Missions' home field, and the home to many barnstorming teams on their stops in the city. The field was famous for a right field fence that was only 250 feet away, an inviting sight for many lefties. The park, made mostly of wood, burned in June of 1933, an hour after a game. All that was saved was the uniforms, bats, balls, and gloves. The Missions finished the rest of the season at tiny Tech Field. The Missions drew an overflowing crowd of 7,850 when they beat the Galveston Buccaneers on September 13, 1933, for the Texas League Championship.

Block Field, across from the old Wheatley High School, also served as a home to the local nine. Minor League teams from the North also used Block Field as a spring training practice site.

Dwight Eisenhower and the
St. Mary's Football Team

Dwight Eisenhower first played football as a youngster in Kansas. Though it was never his life's passion to be a football star, he was a lifelong fan of the game. The young Midwesterner soon became a football star at West Point. In 1912 Eisenhower was a running back on an Army team which included Omar Bradley. He was nicknamed the "Kansas Cyclone," and a *New York Times* correspondent called him one of the most promising backs in the East. An injury during a game against Tufts ended Eisenhower's football career at the academy during his freshman year.

After graduation in 1915, the newly commissioned lieutenant received orders to report to Fort Sam Houston. During the fall of that year, Eisenhower was approached by Peacock Military Academy to coach its football team. The school offered him $150 for the season, a tidy sum considering a lieutenant's pay. At first he refused because he felt, as an Army officer, he would have no time for football. The head of the academy was a friend of post commander General Frank Funston. Funston learned of the offer and asked Eisenhower to accept the offer, citing it would be good for the Army. The new coach won recognition for his handling of the prep stars. A *San Antonio Express* correspondent wrote, "Those who have seen this officer operate with a football squad believe him to be one of the best coaches in Texas — bar none." The Army officer delivered a winning season for the 1915 Peacock Military Academy football team.

The year 1916 brought about a new set of challenges. Eisenhower was now married, and Peacock had acquired a new coach. St. Louis College (now St. Mary's University) was now after Dwight to coach their team. The college team was dreadful. They had not won a game in five years and were coached by a group of priests. Not only did they not win, lopsided scores of 50-0 and 80-0 were common. The small squad tied its first game under Eisenhower, then went on to win its next five games. St Louis lost its last game and finished the season with a record of 5-1-1. Present at every game was the coach's young wife, Mamie. Quarterback Jim Sweeney told the *Express*, "We thought more of him than we did of any other coach we ever had. We respected him from the time he showed up until he left, and we fought as much for Mamie and the Douds (her parents who also attended the games) as we did the school. He was very frank and honest and we learned more about honor and discipline from him than we did anywhere else."

Mamie was the only woman ever to receive a St. Louis or St. Mary's football letter. The fathers were so pleased with the season that they gave the coach and Mamie a victory dinner and a long-lasting relationship between the school and the Eisenhowers developed. The president last visited the school in 1962 to talk to students and faculty. In 1987 David Eisenhower, the former president's grandson, visited the school and discussed his grandfather's connection to the university during the school's annual President's Dinner.

Eisenhower also spent some time helping out with the school's baseball team. Ernest Stecker, a civilian employee, recalled to the *Express* in 1956 how he incurred the wrath of his coach during a close game. St Louis was behind by one run with two men on, and the team's slugger was in the on-deck circle. Stecker received the signal from Eisenhower to bunt but decided to swing away. On the next pitch, Stecker slammed the ball for a triple, but instead of congratulations, all he received was a stern look. He had disobeyed orders.

St. Mary's Football - The Following Years

St Mary's no longer has a football team; football was discontinued prior to World War II. For many years, however, the school had a prominent gridiron history. Probably its most successful period was in the 1930s. From 1935 until 1938 the team was coached by Frank Bridges, the legendary

Baylor coach. In 1935 Doug "Rabbit" Locke was named full-back on the Associated Press All American Team.

In 1939 running back Curt Sandig set a record for a run of 108 yards. Sandig received the ball eight yards deep in the end zone and ran it the length of the field. (Records for rushing have been changed. Running backs are now awarded yards only after the line of scrimmage.) St. Mary's schedule contained some of the powerhouses of the day, including Orange Bowl participants Catholic University, San Francisco, and De Paul. The St. Mary's team became known for tough Texas football and a little bit of showmanship.

Athletic Director Mose Simms was the lifeblood of the team. Simms put up the money for the team and received a portion of the profits. He scoured the state for the best players, promising them a room, education, travel, and all the food they could eat. *Life* magazine ran a feature on him and St. Mary's recruiting efforts on October 16, 1939. The magazine showed the school's legendary double-decker blue bus, which logged an average of 10,000 miles a year, and stated that the school was "well on its way to becoming a football power."

Former *Houston Post* sports editor Clark Nealon, who once covered the school for the *San Antonio Light*, stated that Simms was the best promoter he ever saw, "Compared to him, Roy Hofheinz and Bud Adams are two bit-promoters." One of his greatest stunts was against San Francisco in 1936. Simms had the team practice in old tattered uniforms. He even had the players stumble around during drills which caused hoots and howls from opposing fans and players. Then on game day, the team took the field in brand new uniforms. The home team quickly realized they had been duped. The stunt became one of Simms' most popular.

Herman Richter of Richter's Bakery was a player on Simms' team in the late 1930s. Richter was the only player on the team who was not on scholarship. According to the now prominent businessman, most of the players that Simms recruited were older students (some were even bald), who for some reason or another had dropped out of other schools. Very few were typical student athletes; most came only to play football. During one road trip, the Christian Brothers came to teach the players their lessons. When one reporter came to take a picture of the players studying, some of the so-called student athletes had to grab phone directories because they had not brought any books.

Because of the heavy toll that traveling took on the team, Richter's grades suffered, and his father would not let him play his senior year. But he still has fond memories of Simms; "Simms was quite a talker, he could make you feel like an All American even if you never played the game. He was very likable; if he was alive today he would be something else. When we traveled, Simms wouldn't check out the team, he would count the number of people in the stands."

St. Mary's football was discontinued prior to World War II. The promoter and the Brothers had differences when it came to the team, and the school shut down Mose Simms' traveling road show for good.

The Alamo Bowl

Dallas, Shreveport, and El Paso all host a holiday post-season college bowl game. Unfortunately, San Antonio is left out in the cold when it comes to postseason festivities. With a new downtown domed stadium, San Antonio sports fans have revived hopes that someday a bowl game will be held here. Few sports fans remember that the Alamo City at one time did host such an event.

The year was 1947. Alamo Stadium was the site of the first ever Alamo Bowl. The event was sponsored by the Elks Club, who hoped to raise money for the Crippled Children's Hospital in Ottine. The New Year's Day game was to feature the 11-0 Hardin-Simmons Cowboys, champions of the Border Conference, against the co-Champions of the Big Seven Conference, the 5-4-1 University of Denver Pioneers. (The University of Denver tied with Utah State, who were lucky enough to travel to Fresno for the Raisin Bowl.) The Cowboys were 11-point favorites.

The game met with several difficulties. The day before the contest, San Antonio was hit by its worst ice storm in 100 years. It was the most prolonged freeze since the 1800s; old-timers still talk about it. The police would not allow people to enter the stadium because of the danger of icy steps. The playing field was in equally poor shape, being covered by two inches of ice. The game had to be postponed from Wednesday, January 1, 1947, to Saturday, January 4. Both teams had to stay around town for the contest. Hardin-Simmons worked out at Alamo Heights Stadium, and Denver practiced at Harlandale Stadium.

When Saturday rolled around, the weather had not improved much, which really hurt attendance. A mere 3,730 fans witnessed Hardin-Simmons roll over Denver 20-0. The closest Denver got to the end zone was late in the fourth quarter, when they worked the ball to the five but lost it on downs.

Few sports fans recall the football events of that day. Most of the city was abuzz with the state basketball tournament game between Jefferson and Brackenridge high schools. The Elks Club wound up losing a substantial amount of money on the contest which effectively put an end to the Alamo Bowl, as it faded into obscurity along with the Oil Bowl, the Cigar Bowl, and yes, the Raisin Bowl.

San Antonio's Cotton Bowl Team

Next time you're bellied up to the bar at Little Hipp's (or whatever your favorite watering hole may be), challenge the crowd to this simple question.

The odds are in your favor that someone will owe you a cold one.

Q. Name the only team from San Antonio to appear in the Cotton Bowl.

A. The Randolph Field Ramblers

Never heard of them? Few people remember them. The year was 1943, and World War II was in full swing. Many military posts had athletic teams filled with professional athletes and ex-college greats. Randolph Field was no exception. The Ramblers were stocked with many players who had already used up their college eligibility.

The team was led by former Tulsa All-American quarterback Glenn Dobbs (who also played for the professional Chicago Cardinals before the war). One of Dobbs' favorite receivers was player-coach Major Raymond Morse who had played college ball for Oregon nine years earlier and also had some pro experience. Martin Ruby played on the line for Randolph. Two years earlier, he was rated the best lineman in the Southwest Conference while playing for A&M. The team was coached by Lt. Frank Tritico and had University of Texas baseball great and former coach Bibb A. Falk (as in U.T.'s Disch-Falk Field) as their trainer.

The team was picked to face Texas in the 1944 Cotton Bowl. Both teams had one loss and both teams were relatively close to Dallas. Travel was restricted during the war. The Longhorns, coached by legend Dana X. Bible, were an 8-5 favorite in the contest. Texas had a faster team and deeper reserves. A sellout crowd was expected for the game, and the contest was being broadcast by Mutual overseas for American Armed Forces.

Thirty-two thousand tickets were purchased for the game but only 15,000 people showed up due to a downpour. The game was bogged down by a muddy field. Despite the horrible conditions, Randolph's quarterback Dobbs had a great day, but he only managed to reach paydirt once. The game ended in a 7-7 tie, the first tie in Cotton Bowl history.

Both teams received championship watches. The proceeds that the Randolph team earned went to the Army Air Force Emergency Relief Fund. Texas coach Bible let the Randolph players take the championship trophy home.

One Incredible Round of Golf

When golf fans speak of great rounds of golf, rarely do they mention the greatest professional round ever played. Few people remember the efforts of Mike Souchak and his record breaking score of 257 for 72 holes of golf in 1955—a record that has stood for over 35 years and may never be broken.

The 1955 Texas Open was the oldest tournament on the tour's winter circuit and was played at Brackenridge Golf Course. Many of the tournaments in that day and age were played on municipal courses. On Thursday, February 17, twenty-seven-year-old Mike Souchak, an ex-Duke football star, shot an incredible 60 on the first day. The final nine holes, Souchak shot a record 27 (2,4,4,3,3,3,3,3,2), which stood until 1970. Despite having a fabulous round, the young linkster held only a two-shot lead over Freddie Haas, who shot an equally miraculous 62.

Souchak, who turned pro in 1952 after getting out of the Navy, recorded an impressive 68 on Friday, but Freddie Haas hung in with a 67 and now trailed Souchak by a mere stroke.

On Saturday, rain had caused the condition of the course to deteriorate. Souchak three putted on the 13th hole and lost the lead for a short time. By the end of the day, he was back on top with a round of 64. Despite such a fabulous three days, he still led by a slim margin over Haas.

The final day drew record crowds to Brackenridge. It also drew near-freezing temperatures. On the 18th hole, the jam-packed galley watched Souchak finish with a 65 for the day and a record 257 for the four-day event. After picking up his ball, he yelled to the crowd, "It's been the greatest thrill I've ever had." For his efforts, he picked up a winner's check of $2200. The 1955 Texas Open was his first tour victory.

Freddie Haas' incredible effort tapered off on the final day with a 70, and he finished second with a 261. He took home $1500 and replied that Souchak "will be one of the all-time greats." His prediction never came true. Souchak became a footnote in golf record books. He never did achieve tour stardom. He played on Ryder Cup teams in 1959 and 1961, and his best years on the tour were 1955 to 1961. He never won a major tournament. Other "youngsters" in the tournament did make names for themselves, such as Arnold Palmer and Gene Litler.

As for Brackenridge Golf Course, it has also become a footnote in golf history. Professional golf is rarely played on public courses anymore, and Brackenridge barely resembles the course that hosted the Texas Open in 1955. When McAllister Freeway was built, it cut into the back nine and forever altered the course, making the holes shorter, noisier, and less challenging.

Bowling Ball Mecca

Though few people realize it, San Antonio has become something of a mecca for bowling balls. Columbia 300 Inc., internationally known bowling ball manufacturer, calls San Antonio its home. Its sole plant is located on the north side of San Antonio (5005 West Ave., to be exact). Columbia 300 started in Ephrata, Washington, on the Columbia River and moved to San Antonio when it outgrew its Washington plant.

Columbia is the largest manufacturer of polyester bowling balls in the world and has recently become a leader in the manufacturing of polyurethane resin balls. The Columbia 300 Yellow Dot is the winningest ball in the history of the PBA. The company also has an excellent collection of unusual and commemorative balls it has manufactured. Bowling balls are the company's only product, and they are sold only in pro shops and bowling lanes.

Most San Antonians are unaware that they live in the world's bowling ball mecca. The company prefers it that way, intentionally keeping a low profile to distract competitors in the cut-throat world of bowling ball manufacturing. Plant tours are a rare event, and publicity is almost nonexistent. The plant is situated on a busy San Antonio street, but few realize that the cutting edge of bowling technology is being researched inside.

Six San Antonio Sport Franchises and Their Defunct Leagues

San Antonio Gunslingers - United States Football League

The Gunslingers were probably the worst-run franchise in this early '80s summer football league. While the New Jersey Generals played in the luxurious Meadowlands and had the backing of Donald Trump and players like Doug Flutie, Brian Sipe, and Herschel Walker, the Gunslingers were owned by rancher Clinton Manges and played in half-empty Alamo Stadium. The franchise was the embarrassment of the much-maligned league. The team's offices were in a mobile building in Alamo Stadium's parking lot. During a nationally televised contest on ESPN, there was a power blackout at Alamo Stadium. There were even reports that Trump didn't want his team to play the Gunslingers.

Owner Clinton Manges did not help the image of the franchise. Often the players went unpaid. To this day, some of the players are still owed paychecks. Manges also promised the league that he would expand Alamo Stadium to hold 60,000 in time for the 1986 season. (The stadium, used primarily for high school games, did receive Astroturf and a fresh coat of paint in the Gunslingers' colors of green and blue.) A controversial thirty-year lease, with two ten-year options, was signed.

The team folded, along with the league, after the 1985 season. The USFL tried to save itself by suing the National Football League on antitrust grounds. The USFL won, but it was only awarded three dollars and closed its turnstiles for good.

The San Antonio Wings - World Football League

This ambitious summer league lasted only two seasons: 1974 and 1975. The Wings played in the final season and posted a 7-4-4 record leading the Western Division and a 0-2 record during the fall playoffs. The Wings possessed the league's leading passer, John Walton, who went on to play for the Philadelphia Eagles.

The league lost ten million dollars in 1975 (and a total of thirty million in two years) and it folded on October 2, 1975.

Texas Rowels - Major League Rodeo

San Antonio may have never had a major league baseball team, but it was lucky enough to have a Major League Rodeo team. This unique concept started in the spring of 1978 with six teams. The Western Division included the Denver Stars, the Los Angeles Rough Riders, and the Salt Lake City Buckaroos. The Midwestern Division featured the Kansas City Trailblazers, the Tulsa Twisters, and the Texas Rowels, who hailed from San Antonio. (A rowel is the freewheeling part of the spur.)

Major League Rodeo consisted of seven traditional events: team roping, bareback riding, saddle bronc riding, calf roping, steer wrestling, bull riding, and barrel racing, which was an "all cowgirl event."

Major League Rodeo had a cable television contract but failed anyway in the early 1980s.

San Antonio Cavaliers - National Bowling League

The Alamo City has the distinction of being one of the few cities ever to have its own team, the San Antonio Cavaliers, in the National Bowling League. This ill-fated concept lasted one season. The league had five-man teams bowling head to head in a two-game series. One point was awarded for each win and a bonus point awarded for scores over 210. Every ten pins would add another bonus point and ten bonus points were awarded for a 300 game. Minimum salary for bowlers was $6000.

The league had ten teams. Surely you recall most of them: Dallas Bronchos, Detroit Thunderbirds, Ft. Worth Panthers, Fresno Bombers, Kansas City Stars, Omaha Packers, Los Angeles Toros, New York Gladiaters (actually Totowa, N.J.), Twin Cities Skippers, and the San Antonio Cavaliers.

The season ran from October 12, 1961, until May 6, 1962. Unfortunately, the era of team bowling was ending and the advent of the Professional Bowlers Tour was beginning. The San Antonio Cavaliers fared little better than the league. The Cavaliers had no home lanes and operated solely as a road club. It folded on December 17, 1961. Only six teams would finish the season. In 1962, due to poor attendance and fan disinterest, the league passed into oblivion.

San Antonio Thunder - North American Soccer League

This league was formed in 1968 with the merger of the National Professional Soccer League and the United Soccer Association. The San Antonio Thunder were in the league for one year in 1976 before moving to Honolulu and becoming Team Hawaii. The NASL folded after the 1984 season.

San Antonio Spurs - American Basketball Association

The Spurs are still around, but the ABA is long gone. The Spurs were originally the Dallas Chaparrals and moved to Hemisfair Arena for the 1973 season. The ABA is still fondly remembered for the red, white, and blue basketball, the original three-point shot, and the playing of such greats as Julius Erving, Moses Malone, and George Gervin.

The Dallas Chaparrals never found success in big D, but they were a huge hit in the Alamo City. The newly reborn San Antonio Spurs played their first game in October, 1973. The silver and black were runners-up for the ABA title in 1974. After the 1975-1976 season, the Spurs, along with the Denver Nuggets, New York Nets (now New Jersey), and the Indiana Pacers, were asked to join the National Basketball Association. The remaining teams (the Kentucky Colonels, Virginia Squires, and the Spirit of St. Louis) followed the ABA and the red, white, and blue ball into oblivion.

The Spurs immediately prospered in the NBA, coming within one game in 1979 of the NBA finals. The roof of Hemisfair Arena was raised in 1977 to accommodate an upper deck and increased seating from 10,100 to over 15,000. (If you look closely enough on the outside of the arena, you will notice that the bricks about halfway up are a tad different. The late addition of the upper deck is also the reason the arena has a number of posts throughout the lower deck that obstruct the view of many fans.)

The Spurs are the only franchise in the city's history to actually outlive its league. The team has had a number of great players, including James Silas (#13) and George Gervin (#44), both of whom have had their numbers retired. Gervin is perhaps the most colorful player in the history of the franchise. He was known as the "Iceman" because he always remained cool and it was said he had ice water in his veins. Ironically, Gervin's trademark coolness did not develop in his college days. As a player for the Eastern Michigan University Hurons, the young Gervin punched a player during a postseason game in 1972. He left the university soon after but was later honored by the school when they retired his jersey.

"The opera ain't over till the fat lady sings."
Dan Cook, *Express-News* columnist
and KENS sportscaster

SECTION VI

SAN ANTONIO NAMES

Names

San Antonio — The river (and subsequently the city) was named for St. Anthony de Padua, because the river was discovered on his day, June 13, 1691, by Spanish explorers. Dom Domingo de Teras, governor of the New Phillippines (as Texas was called then), and Padre Damian Masanet, senior chaplain, were both with the expedition party that discovered the river, and both claim in their journals that they are responsible for the name.

Bexar County — On May 5, 1718, Spanish Governor Martin de Alarcon proclaimed the establishment on the river as the Royal Presidio of San Antonio de Bejar, named in honor of the saint and of the Duque de Bejar, a brother of the viceroy, who had been killed in Hungary fighting the Turks.

Castroville — This small South Texas town is named after Henri Castro, who was born in France of Portuguese Jewish parents. Castro served on Napoleon's Guard of Honor, fought to defend Paris in 1814, and was an officer in the Legion of Honor in 1818. While in Texas in 1842, Castro entered into a contract with the Texan government to settle a colony of French immigrants. The town was founded in 1844, mainly by families from the province of Alsace in France.

Mission San Antonio de Valero — The Alamo as it was originally known was named by Father Olivares in honor of the viceroy, Malques de Valero.

San Pedro Springs — Named by Father Isidro Felix de Espinosa on April 13, 1709, when the expedition discovered the springs. The springs are named for Saint Peter or San Pedro.

The Henry B. Gonzales Convention Center — This massive downtown complex is named in honor of longtime San Antonio congressman Henry B. Gonzales. Gonzales, a former San Antonio city councilman and the first Hispanic member of Congress, is best known for his long speeches on a variety of topics and for punching out a man twenty years his junior at Earl Abel's Restaurant.

Lila Cockrell Theatre — Named after the city's first woman mayor. The two-time mayor also has an apartment complex for the elderly named after her.

Arneson River Theatre — Named after E. P. Arneson, the first consulting engineer on the River Walk, who died in 1938, before construction got underway.

Callaghan Road — named after longtime San Antonio mayor Bryan Callaghan, who served the city from 1885 to 1899 and from 1905 to 1912, when he died in office.

Eisenhauer Road — It's not named after the former president, but for Otto Eisenhauer, the son of a German immigrant who farmed on the northeast side for nearly seventy years.

Jones-Maltsberger Road — This road once led to two dairies, one owned by the Jones family and the other owned by the Maltsberger family.

Rittiman Road and Walzem Road also are names of roads that once led to family-owned dairies.

Perrin-Beitel Road — This road led to land owned by two families, the Perrins and the Beitels. Near the main post office on Perrin-Beitel is an old family cemetery for the two landowners.

West Avenue, DeZavala, Evers, Eckert, Babcock, Huebner, and Marbach roads are all named for families who built the roads out to their land.

McCullough Avenue — Named after Reverend John McCullough of First Presbyterian Church in San Antonio in

1846. The road helped to bring people from the north side to the downtown church.

Belknap Street — Named after Augustus Belknap, who put in the city's first streetcars, which were mule-driven down San Pedro Avenue.

Brees Boulevard — Named for Lt. General Herbert J. Brees who was commander of the Third Army headquartered in the Smith-Young Tower (now the Tower Life Building). Brees was stationed in San Antonio from October 1940 to May 1941.

Flores Street — One of the oldest streets in San Antonio, this thoroughfare was named in honor of Nicolas Flores y Valdez, who fought against Indian raids during the Aguayo Expedition in 1817. The expedition fought to open supply routes to the area's missions. Some sources say this street was named Flores Street (meaning flowers in Spanish) simply because of the many flowers that grew along the boulevard.

Travis, Crockett, Bowie, Bohnam, and Milam Streets — All were named after the heroes of the Alamo.

St. Mary's Street — named in honor of the Brothers of St. Mary's, who came to San Antonio in 1851 to start St. Mary's University.

Main Avenue — Originally named Acequia Street, the name was changed to Main Avenue because it was often referred to as Main Street. Many called it Main Street because Main High School was located on the avenue.

College Street — This downtown street was so named because it ran by St. Mary's College. The school has since been moved to the northwest side of town, and La Mansion Hotel now occupies the site.

Soledad Street — At one time, this street had only one house on it, so it was named Soledad, Spanish for lonely.

Convent Street — named for the Ursuline nuns, whose convent was located on the street. The building is now home to the Southwest Craft Center.

Dolorosa Street — Dolorosa is Spanish, meaning street of sadness. There are three different explanations as to why this street is named Dolorosa. Some sources say it was named for the Virgin Mary, mother of sadness. Others say it was named the street of sadness because it led to Mexico, and many wives saw their soldier husbands leave town on the road, never to return.

A third story says the avenue was named street of sadness in reference to mourners who witnessed a mass execution on Military Plaza in the early 1800s.

Kenmore Street — This small street once separated Sears from its parking garage and is named for the store's line of appliances.

Jack White Street — This small street between Nueva and Villita streets was originally built by the Plaza Hotel (now Grenada Homes) as a place for cabs to park and for motorists to turn around. The street was unnamed for many years and caused a problem for the hotel's proprietor, who had trouble giving directions to the business located on the end of the nameless avenue. The hotel operator was named, you guessed it, Jack White.

Jack White, one of the first proponents of the River Walk, later became mayor of San Antonio, thereby acquiring the influence to have the street named after himself.

Broadway — This avenue originally had three names: Avenue C, Lasoya, and River Avenue. The street received the name Broadway at the suggestion of Alamo Heights residents, who thought the street that led to their enclave should have an exceptional name.

Navarro Street — Named after Jose Antonio Navarro, one of the signers of the Texas Declaration of Independence.

Nogalitos Street — Meaning "little pecan trees" in Spanish, this street was once lined with such flora.

Zarzamora Street — Spanish, meaning thorny mulberries. The Spanish who settled San Antonio discovered dewberries on the site. Not knowing what they were, they assumed they were some sort of thorny mulberry and named the street after the bushes on the side of the road.

Presa Street — This street once led to Espada Dam and was named for its destination. Presa is Spanish for dam.

King's Highway — This picturesque avenue on the city's near north side is anything but a highway. It was named after the ancient El Camino Real (Spanish for King's Highway), a road built to connect the missions of Texas. One hundred and twenty-three markers throughout Texas designate the course of the road. One marker rests in San Pedro Park and was dedicated on March 2, 1920.

Charles Anderson Loop (aka Loop 1604) — The city's outer loop bears the name of a former Bexar County judge. The honorable Charles Anderson served twenty-five years on the bench, despite having to walk on crutches after losing part of his foot in World War II. Anderson died of cancer in 1964.

Josephine Tobin Drive — This small stretch of road that snakes around Woodlawn Lake and is introduced via an expansive sign is named after the only woman who was both a mother and a daughter to a San Antonio mayor. She was the mother of Mayor John Tobin and the daughter of Mayor John William Smith.

Harry Wurzbach Road — Named after four-term U.S. Congressman Harry Wurzbach, who served in the House from 1921 until 1932. Wurzbach was also a corporal in the First Texas Volunteer Infantry, a four-term county judge, and a one-time county attorney. Wurzbach drew his support from the area's large German population, which made him a virtual shoe-in for congressman. He was the first Republican congressman from Texas to be elected for more than two terms to the House. Born on May 19, 1874, he died November 6, 1931. Wurzbach is buried in the forgotten U.S. Cemetery on the city's east side.

Michael Nesmith Street — This avenue in a subdivision in Leon Valley is named after the former Monkees rock group member. Nesmith lived in San Antonio for a time and attended San Antonio College. The street was named by Nesmith's uncle, who was one of the developers of Leon Valley.

George Gervin Court — This small street in front of Hemisfair Arena is named for Spurs basketball great, number 44, George Gervin. Gervin, whose retired number hangs from the arena, was one of the greatest players ever to don a Spurs uniform.

General McMullen Drive — Named for a former commander of Kelly Air Force Base.

Cupples Road — This road is named after Colonel Cupples, a former agent of Henri Castro.

Basse Road — Named for Edgar A. Basse, Sr., founder of the Piggly Wiggly supermarket chain.

Bandera Road — Many roads were named because of where they lead. Bandera road led to Bandera, Blanco Road led to Blanco, Fredricksburg Road led to that small town, and it's obvious where Austin Highway led to. When the interstate highway system was completed, many of the roads were incorporated into the highway, and now they no longer lead all the way to their respective towns.

Other roads named after the towns they led to include New Braunfels, Nacogdoches, Pleasanton, Wetmore, Corpus Christi, and Somerset roads.

Stinson Field — The small municipal airport located on the city's south side is named for the Stinson family, who operated a flying school there in the 1910s. The airport is one of the three oldest in the U.S.

The airport was renamed Windburn Field after a plane crash on October 15, 1927, took the life of *San Antonio Express* reporter Bill Windburn. On July 15, 1936, the field was renamed Stinson Field.

During World War II, Stinson Field was taken over by the Army Air Corps for pilot training. Interestingly enough, Marjorie Stinson trained World War I pilots at the same field when it was her private flying school almost thirty years earlier.

Kelly AFB — Named for Army Lt. George E. M. Kelly, who died in a plane crash at Fort Sam Houston May 10, 1911. Kelly was the first military pilot to lose his life in a plane accident. Because of his death, all military flights were halted for three years. Kelly is buried in San Antonio in the first military cemetery, located in the city's eastside cemetery complex. Kelly received his commission and his wings posthumously.

Brooks AFB — Named for Cadet Sidney Johnston Brooks, Jr., the first San Antonio native to lose his life in a World War I related activity. Brooks died on November 13, 1917, after apparently fainting on return from a training flight from Hondo Air Field to Kelly Field. Brooks is buried in San Antonio but not in the U.S. Cemetery. To find his grave site, look for the western edge of the city's eastside cemetery complex, off Commerce Street. The Brooks family plots are located across from Clara Driscoll's tomb.

Randolph AFB — Named for Captain William M. Randolph, who was killed in a plane crash at Kelly Field (some reports say Gorman Field) in 1928. Randolph was on the committee that helped design the base.

Lackland AFB — Named for General Frank D. Lackland, who was the pioneer commander of Kelly Field. Originally, the area now occupied by Lackland AFB was a bombing range for Kelly. After Pearl Harbor, it became the San Antonio Cadet Center. In 1947 it became Lackland AFB.

Wilford Hall Medical Center — Named in 1963 for Major General Wilford Hall, who was stationed at Randolph Field in the 1930s. Dr. Hall was a pioneer in the field of aviation surgery.

Fort Sam Houston — Named after the general who led Texas troops to victory over Santa Anna in the Battle of San Jacinto. The military hero, and soon to be Texas governor, captured Santa Anna in eighteen minutes.

Brooke Army Medical Center — Originally named Brooke General Hospital, it was named in honor of Brigadier General Roger Brooke, the former commanding officer at the old post hospital. The hospital opened in 1937, at a cost of two million dollars. Fort Sam is now home to the military's finest burn facility and the U.S. Army's medical school.

Dizzy Dean Field — This baseball field at Fort Sam Houston is named after the former major league pitcher who served in the Army at Fort Sam Houston during World War II. During his time here, he found some spare time to play for the post's baseball team.

Dodd Field — These athletic grounds at Fort Sam were originally used as a testing field for airplanes during the first World War. It was named after Captain Townsend F. Dodd, who died in a military plane crash.

Funston Loop — This Fort Sam street, with some of the most picturesque homes in the city (not to mention some of the most beautiful military quarters ever), is named after General Frederick Funston, commander of the post from 1915 until his death in 1917.

Camp Bullis — Named for General John Lapham Bullis, who in 1873 took command of a company of Seminole Indians and defended settlers against Indian raids. Bullis died on May 26, 1911, and is buried in the U.S. Cemetery on the city's east side.

Audie Murphy Memorial Veterans Hospital — There was a time when every American knew of the exploits of Audie Murphy. A new generation of Americans has come of age that has never read of a young Texas boy who became the most decorated soldier of World War II. Murphy won twelve medals of valor, including the Distinguished

Service Cross and the Congressional Medal of Honor, the nation's two highest awards. The story of a young soldier from Greenville, Texas, who had killed 240 Germans, ended up in *Life Magazine*, and Audie Murphy became a national icon. After the war, Murphy headed to Hollywood, where he starred in mostly westerns and war movies (including his autobiography). He died in a plane crash in 1971.

The Judge John H. Wood Courthouse — This circular building on Hemisfair Plaza was originally the U.S. Pavilion for the World's Fair. After the event, it became a courthouse. It was eventually renamed for Judge John Wood, who was killed in June of 1979, by a single bullet, while leaving his San Antonio home for work one morning. He was the first federal judge murdered in more than a century. Known as "Maximum John" because of his strict punishments, the judge was feared by many involved in drug trafficking. At the time of the murder, Wood was scheduled to preside over the trial of reputed drug lord Jimmy Chagra.

An interesting note: The man convicted of murdering the judge was John Harrelson. His son Woody Harrelson stars as Woody on the popular TV show "Cheers."

Mayor Maury Maverick Plaza — This open space in La Villita is named in honor of the mayor who organized the restoration of La Villita. A bust of the mayor is on display in front of the plaza on Alamo Street.

O'Neil Ford Plaza — This small, forgotten place behind the Little Church of La Villita is named for the architect of the restoration of La Villita. Ford was one of the city's most noted architects; he was one of the first to be concerned with the conservation of historic structures. Some of his most notable works include Trinity University and the Tower of the Americas.

The Rose Window — The San Jose Mission, built in 1720, is known for its beautiful Rose Window. The name of the delicate stone carved window frame is somewhat of a mystery, because there are no roses whatsoever on the piece.

The name was given by its sculptor, Pedro Huizar, who crafted the piece for his love, a woman named Rosa.

First-time visitors to San Jose Mission may find the Rose Window to be somewhat familiar. Replicas of the frame were made for the display windows at the downtown Joske's (now Dillards at Rivercenter).

Main Plaza or Plaza de las Islas — Spanish for Plaza of the Islands, this downtown park across from the courthouse was named for the first settlers of San Antonio from the Canary Islands.

Military Plaza — City Hall now sits on Military Plaza, which was once the social center of downtown. Chili queens, merchants, and a variety of characters gathered there throughout the 1800s. It received its name from the previous century, when it had barracks for a garrison on the north side of the plaza.

The east side of the plaza was designated for the Catholic church (San Fernando Cathedral is situated on the east side), the west side was set aside for civil and military officials (the Spanish Governor's Palace sits on the west side), and the south side was reserved for settlers.

Brackenridge Park — Named for George Brackenridge, one of San Antonio's greatest philanthropists. Brackenridge started one of San Antonio's first financial institutions, the city's water system, and worked to develop the public school system. The land that is now the park was donated by Brackenridge. A statue of the man who is perhaps the city's greatest patriarch stands at the Broadway entrance to the park. The park opened in 1900.

Milam Park — This downtown plaza, sandwiched between Santa Rosa Hospital and El Mercado, is named after Ben Milam, who came to Texas in 1818 and was active in the Texas Revolution. He died in 1835, when he was hit by a sniper's bullet. The bridge on the River Walk behind the Petroleum Commerce building has a mural depicting the killing of Ben Milam.

Milam Park is unique because it is actually a cemetery. Milam is buried on the west end of the block-long park, while some of the original Canary Islanders are buried on the east side.

Mahncke Park — This small and mostly undeveloped park situated at Broadway and Funston Place provides a pleasant green space amidst the hustle of Broadway. The park is named for Ludwig Mahncke, the first park commissioner for the city. Mahncke was instrumental in securing the donation of land for Brackenridge Park.

Lambert Beach — The north end of Brackenridge Park is known as Lambert Beach. At one time this was a popular swimming spot on the San Antonio River. The changing rooms are still in existence next to the zoo fence. Lambert Beach is named for Ray Lambert, a popular park commissioner from the 1920s who was responsible for the Sunken Gardens.

McAllister Park/McAllister Freeway — Both were named for former mayor W. W. McAllister and the founder of San Antonio Savings. The mayor was instrumental in getting U.S. 281 built as a passageway to the north side.

O. P. Schnabel Park — This city park was named after the founder of the Beautify San Antonio Association and the Beautify Texas Council. Though Schnabel died in 1987, the namesake park was established when he was still living (see entry O. P. Schnabel).

Koehler Park — This park adjacent to Brackenridge Park (few people realize that they are actually two parks) was donated to the city in 1915, by Emma Koehler, former president of the Pearl Brewing Company.

The Koehler estate (now the Koehler Cultural Center), a block-long residence adjacent to San Antonio College, is now used by the school.

Various city parks are named after people who donated land to the city simply because they wanted a park in their neighborhood. They include Raymond Russell Park (donated by Meta and Raymond Russell in 1951), Pletz Park (donated by Leo Pletz in 1963), and Orsinger Park (donated by Ward and Genevieve Orsinger in 1980).

Koger Stokes Softball Center — This complex located in San Pedro Park is named after the organizer and former president of the Texas Amateur Athletic Foundation.

Dignowity Park — Also known as Dignowity Hill. The hill was named for the Dignowity family, who had built a large home dubbed "Harmony House" in this once prominent eastside neighborhood. The house was torn down in 1926, and the land is now a city park.

The head of the family was Czechoslovakian Dr. Anthony M. Dignowity, who came to America in 1832, after participating in a failed Polish revolt against Russia. He studied medicine in Mississippi before settling in San Antonio. With the approaching Civil War, the young doctor became quite vocal in his opposition to slavery. He fled to the North when concerns for his safety grew. When he returned to San Antonio in 1869, he found that his assets had been seized. He died in 1875, after spending his last six years trying to recover his property.

The eastside Dignowity neighborhood received historic designation in 1985. The neighborhood is older than the King William neighborhood, and it was the first fashionable area outside of the city's core. In the nineteenth century, the area was a haven for the rich who wanted to escape the hustle and bustle of San Antonio.

King William District — This historic neighborhood just south of downtown was once the bastion of wealthy Germans who settled in San Antonio in the nineteenth century. The area became known as the King Wilhelm neighborhood after King Wilhelm I of Prussia, who later became a German emperor.

St. Peter Claver Church and the Healy-Murphy Center — This Catholic church on San Antonio's east side is named for a Jesuit missionary who worked in South America with

African slaves. Peter Claver was canonized in 1888, and the chapel built that same year was the first church in the U.S. to be named for him. The parish was the first one for African Americans in this part of Texas.

The parish had been under the supervision of the Josephite Fathers until 1964, when the parish became affiliated with St. Joseph's. St. Peter Claver Academy, adjacent to the church, is now home to Healy-Murphy Learning Center and Child Care Center. It is partially named for Mrs. Margaret Murphy, a widow of a former Corpus Christi mayor who founded the academy. Mrs. Murphy devoted her time and money to serving poor African Americans after hearing a sermon denouncing the practice of having non-whites sit at the back of the church.

Little Flower Church — This Catholic church was named for Sister Therese, a Carmelite nun, who was known as the Little Flower. Known as the Shrine of the Little Flower, the church is officially known as the Parish of Our Lady of Mount Carmel and St. Therese.

Joe and Harry Freeman Coliseum — The coliseum was given the name Joe Freeman Coliseum, after the stock show and rodeo founder Joe Freeman, who died in 1975. The name was later changed to the Joe and Harry Freeman Coliseum after his brother Harry, a lifelong stock show board member, died in 1985.

The facility was originally named the Bexar County Coliseum and opened October 19, 1949.

Blossom Athletic Center — This complex, which consists of various athletic facilities for the Northeast Independent School District, is named in honor of Virgil T. Blossom, a former superintendent, who died in 1965. Blossom was instrumental in initiating growth in the fledgling district but is better known for his school integration plan in Little Rock, Arkansas. The plan was opposed by the Arkansas governor, who sent National Guardsmen to guard Little Rock's Central High School. Then-president Eisenhower used federal troops to enforce Blossom's plan.

Paul Taylor Field House — This Northside Independent School District gymnasium is named after a popular Northside coach who died of cancer.

Leal Middle School — This southside school is named after Armando Leal, who graduated from Harlandale High School in 1964 and died in Vietnam in 1967, while trying to save wounded Marines.

Churchill High School — This Northeast high school is named after the British chief of state because a former school board member had a particular fondness for Churchill. The Northeast School District has a policy of naming their high schools after famous Americans, but Churchill slipped by because trustee Maxwell Higginbothan argued that since Churchill's mother was American, so was he.

Gus Garcia Junior High — Garcia was the first Mexican-American elected to the San Antonio School District's board of trustees, but he gained fame for bringing suit in U.S. District Court which resulted in the ruling that segregation of Hispanic students was illegal.

Wren Junior High — This school is named after Elizabeth T. Wren, the district's first black teacher.

McFarlin Tennis Center — This first-class tennis facility in San Pedro Park was named after John McFarlin, a millionaire who supported the Trinity University intercollegiate tennis program and helped them to achieve national prominence.

Bowen's Island — This small island in the San Antonio River, located across from the City Public Service Building, was named after its onetime owner John Bowen, the city's first postmaster. At one time, the island was six acres long and was bounded by the river on three sides and the Concepcion Acequia on the other. Bowen bought the island in 1845, from Josefa Rodriguez de Yturri for $300, and built a seven-room house there. Bowen was a staunch Unionist, and his family claims that he hid fugitive slaves at his home. After his death in 1867, Bowen was buried on the island.

family claims that he hid fugitive slaves at his home. After his death in 1867, Bowen was buried on the island.

In 1869 the ditch was filled in to make the island more of a peninsula. Throughout the years, the island has had many owners, including for a short time Daniel Boone. In 1870 it became home to a private garden, and the German athletic club known as the Turn Verein which performed there. The island became a popular gathering spot and a center for social activities. With the rerouting of the river, the island eventually shrunk to its present minuscule size. The Tower Life Building, Granada Homes, and City Public Service Building sit on land that was originally Bowen's Island.

Witte Museum — Named for Alfred G. Witte, who left the city $65,000 in his will to construct a museum in Brackenridge Park. The museum opened in October of 1926.

McNay Art Museum — Originally a mansion owned by Marion Koogler McNay, the home was donated with the express purpose of becoming a museum.

The Hertzberg Circus Collection — This collection of over 20,000 circus items is named after local lawyer Harry Hertzberg. Hertzberg was an avid circus fan, who donated his personal collection of mementos to the city in 1940.

Luby's Cafeterias — Named after co-founder of the cafeteria chain, Robert M. Luby.

Nix Medical Center — This downtown medical landmark is named after J. M. Nix, the builder who constructed South Texas' first major medical complex in November of 1930. Nix also built the Majestic Building, among other downtown properties.

Book Building — This recently renovated historic building is named after Dana Book, a civil engineer, who raised the office structure in 1906. Book came from New York City, where he was instrumental in the construction of that city's subway system.

The Jersey Lilly Saloon — Located in the Pearl Brewery, this facility was named after the original Jersey Lilly Saloon in Langtry, where Judge Roy Bean dispensed both drinks and justice in the late 1800s. The original Jersey Lilly was named after British actress Lillie Langtry, for whom Bean carried a torch.

Club Giraud — This private club on the grounds of the Southwest Craft Center is named after Francois Giraud, the architect who designed the buildings for their original use, the old Ursuline convent.

SECTION VII

SAN ANTONIO FIRSTS

Firsts

First City Charter — San Antonio de Bexar was first granted a charter by the Spanish Crown in 1733.

First non-Military or Religious Settlers — In March of 1731, fifty-six men, women, and children arrived in San Antonio. At the time, the area was occupied mainly by missionaries and soldiers. The Canary Islanders were brought by royal edict from Spain and were destined to become the city's first foothold on civilization. It took one year for the pioneers to travel from the coast of Africa to Mexico, then across land to San Antonio.

First Park — San Pedro Park has the distinction of being the second oldest park in the United States. (Boston Commons was the first.) In 1729 the Spanish King Phillip V, via his viceroy in Mexico, declared the grounds at the head-waters of the springs an Elido or Public Land.

Travis Park was the second park in the city and is the third oldest in the country.

First Fire Department — San Antonio's first fire department was a volunteer group formed with German acrobats from the Turn Verein.

First Museum — The city's first museum, a Museum of Natural History, was built in 1885 in San Pedro Park.

First Symphony — The first symphony orchestra in Texas was formed in San Antonio in 1847.

First Hispanic City Councilman — Elected in 1953, Henry B. Gonzales was the city's first Hispanic city councilman. Gonzales became the first Mexican-American ever elected to the state senate in 1956. In 1961 he was elected to the U.S.

House of Representatives, the first Hispanic to sit among that prestigious body.

First Hispanic Mayor — Elected in 1981, Henry Cisneros became the city's first Mexican-American mayor and the first Hispanic to lead a city the size of San Antonio.

First Woman Mayor — Lila Cockrell was the first woman mayor in San Antonio's history. She was elected twice, the term before Henry Cisneros and the term after.

First Public Housing Project — The first public housing project in the city was the Apache-Alazon Courts on the city's west side. This was also the first public housing project in the nation.

First City to Desegregate — San Antonio desegregated its schools and city facilities in 1954, with the lobbying efforts of then-city councilman Henry B. Gonzales. The city was the first in Texas, and one of the first in the South, to open the doors to all.

First Chinese School — The first Chinese school in Texas was established in San Antonio in 1922. It was located at 215 San Saba.

First Chinese Baptist Church — The church located on Avenue B near the Valero Building was the first of its kind in the South. It first opened its doors in 1923.

First Episcopal Church — St. Mark's Episcopal Church, adjacent to Travis Park, was the city's first Episcopal church. The cornerstone was laid by Lt. Colonel Robert E. Lee in 1859. Construction of the church was halted in 1861 because of the Civil War.

The half-completed structure was often mistaken for an old mission. The chapel was finally completed in 1874. The bell for the church was cast in Troy, New York. The metal was from a cannon used at the Alamo.

First Jewish Congregation — The Temple Beth-El, organized in San Antonio in 1874, was the city's first synagogue. Its first temple was located near Travis Park and constructed in 1875. Its present site near San Antonio College was built in 1933.

First Catholic Church — Mission San Antonio de Valero was founded on May 1, 1718, about two miles south of San Pedro Springs. The mission, known today as the Alamo, moved to its present site in 1724.

First Showing of the Film *The Alamo* — The premiere of *The Alamo*, starring John Wayne, took place at the Woodlawn Theatre on Fredricksburg Road. The theatre no longer shows films and is now a church.

First Movie About the Alamo — Different sources claim two movies as the original Alamo film. Some sources credit *The Fall of the Alamo*, made by the Star Film Company in 1911. The Star Film Company was based at the Hot Wells Hotel. Other sources credit a French company for making a film in 1911, titled *The Immortal Alamo*. The French film used extras from the nearby Peacock Military Academy.

First Academy Awarding Winning Film — The film *Wings* filmed in San Antonio and premiering at the Texas Theatre on May 19, 1927, was the first film ever to win an Academy Award for best picture.

First Oil Production — Forty-nine barrels of oil pumped from George Dullnig's ranch was the first black gold to be produced in Texas. Dullnig's ranch was near the present site of Brooks AFB. A plaque commemorating this first is located on S.E. Military Drive near Goliad Road.

First Streetcars — Mule-driven streetcars first appeared on the city's roadways in June of 1878, taking visitors from downtown to San Pedro Park, then on the outskirts of the city.

In 1890 the first electric streetcars arrived in San Antonio.

First Railroad — February 16, 1877, was the date the first train rolled into town. The Galveston, Harrisburg and San Antonio Railway chugged into the city on the newly created

Sunset Line. The railway is now known as the Southern Pacific.

First Airplane Flight — Lieutenant Benjamin Foulois of the U.S. Army was the first to become airborne in San Antonio. March 2, 1910, at 9:30 A.M., the young Army pilot catapulted his Wright Brothers Flyer above the Arthur MacArthur parade ground on Ft. Sam Houston, not only beginning the era of military flight, but also giving birth to the U.S. Air Force.

First Airport — Early flights in San Antonio took off from the parade ground at Ft. Sam Houston. In 1915, after an appeal by aviatrix Marjorie Stinson, the city opened Stinson Field on the city's southwest side. The field is still in use and is one of the three oldest airports in the nation.

First Air Mail — Marjorie Stinson flew the first air mail route in Texas on February 6, 1928, delivering mail between the municipalities of San Antonio and Seguin, a grand total of thirty miles.

First Women Soldiers — The First Company of the Women's Army Auxiliary Corps was stationed at Fort Sam Houston in 1942. A plaque at the site where their barracks once stood honors these military pioneers.

First Service Clubs — The Rotary Club first organized in San Antonio in June of 1912, with ten members. Herbert J. Hays was the first president.

The Lions Club was first formed locally on January 17, 1919, with twenty-one members, and William L. Stiles as the first president.

First Public Junior College in Texas — San Antonio College was the first public junior college in Texas, opening in 1926 and occupying the old German-English School on South Alamo. The college moved to its present location on San Pedro in 1951.

First Boarding School for Girls — Established in 1851, Ursuline Academy was the first boarding school for girls in San Antonio and the second in Texas.

First Public Secondary School — Main Avenue High School opened in 1879 as the city's first public high school. It was razed in 1917. Fox Technical High School now sits at the site.

First City Team to Win a State Championship — The 1926 Brackenridge Eagles men's basketball team, coached by D. C. "Bobby" Cannon, was the first city team to win a state title for schoolboy sports. The team went undefeated until it lost in the national tournament to a team from Kansas City. The team ended up fourth in the 1926 national tourney. The team was unique because it played its home games on an outdoor hardwood court, believed to be the only one in the nation.

First College Team to Win an NCAA Championship — In 1972 the Tigers from Trinity University won the NCAA Tennis Championship.

First Championship Baseball Team — The San Antonio entry in the Texas League first won the Texas League pennant in 1897.

First Radio Broadcast of Local Baseball Game — In 1929 Earl Wilson of KTAP radio was the first to broadcast a local game.

First Radio Station — WOAI-AM radio was the city's first station, signing on with 500 watts on September 25, 1922. KTSA signed on February 19, 1928, broadcasting from the Plaza Hotel (now the Granada Homes). KABC signed on later that year on December 1 from the Majestic Building, followed shortly by KONO radio, which had its programming originate from the Bluebonnet Hotel.

First Television Station — WOAI-TV Channel 4 was San Antonio's first television station, signing on December 11, 1949. There were approximately twenty-five TV sets in existence in the city. Originally, the station broadcast from 11 A.M. to 10:15 P.M. The station changed its call letters to KMOL in 1975. The station, however, is still located at its original location of 1031 Navarro Street. Channel 4 was also the first television station to run Hollywood movies and to broadcast a church service.

A CBS station, KENS, signed on in 1950, and an ABC station, KONO-TV later KSAT, hit the airwaves in 1957.

First Television Newscaster — In the early days of WOAI-TV, the 10 o'clock news was simulcast with WOAI Radio. Henry Guerra, Frank Mathews, and Jim Metcalf were the first TV anchormen in San Antonio. Guerra, a prominent citizen, can still be heard on WOAI radio. Few people know that besides being a pioneer broadcaster, Guerra is also a local undertaker. Phil Hemphill was the first television weatherman. In the mid-60s, Martha Buchanan became Channel 4's first on-camera newswoman and the first female anchor in Texas.

First Newspaper — In 1849 *The Western Texian* was first printed here, becoming the city's first newspaper.

First Telegraph — Telegraph arrived in the city in 1876. It was used primarily to connect San Antonio with other military centers.

First Telephone — The first telephone in San Antonio was installed on March 22, 1878, from the waterworks to the mayor's office. The first phone in Texas had been installed in Galveston only four days earlier.

There is some speculation that George Brackenridge had the first phone line in the country installed some years earlier from his home to his downtown bank. A *San Antonio Express* article from June 11, 1893, states that Brackenridge had constructed a telephone line between the two locations twenty years earlier. The article states that other cities regarded Brackenridge's telephone as a fad.

First For-Profit Hospital — The Nix Hospital opened in November 1930 at its present location downtown, marking a new era in hospital care. The twenty-four-story structure had the distinction of being the only building in America that housed a hospital, doctors' offices, and a parking garage.

First Two-Story Building — In 1780 Pedro Fuentes built a two-story building on Flores Street, the first in San Antonio.

First Elevator — The Kampmann Building, the city's first four-story building, was also the first building to be equipped with an elevator. The building was constructed in 1883.

First Brewery — William Menger opened the first brewery in the Alamo City in 1855. It was also the first brewery in Texas.

First National Bank — George Brackenridge opened the city's first national bank in 1866. The San Antonio National Bank was located at 239 East Commerce in a building that is now occupied by lawyers' offices.

Brackenridge lived in the adjacent building, and legend has it that the noted philanthropist kept a cow on the roof in order to guarantee a supply of fresh milk.

First Mexican Restaurant — Located at 231 Losoya, the original Mexican restaurant was aptly titled "The Original Mexican Restaurant." Operated by the Farnsworth family, it opened in 1899; before that, Mexican food was sold mainly in open-air markets. The restaurant closed in 1961 and reopened on the River Walk in the 1980s.

First Luby's Cafeteria — The beginning of Luby's Cafeterias started in the basement of a hotel on College and Presa streets. That location is now occupied by the Bayous Restaurant.

First Sears Store — The city's first outlet for this nation-wide superstore opened on March 7, 1929, in the Smith-Young Tower (now the Tower Life Building).

First Sporting Goods Store — The first sporting goods store in Texas was Potchernicks, established in 1894. The company still exists with a store at Loop 410 and Perrin-Beitel. The sign from the original store is on display there.

First Santikos Theatre — Louis Santikos bought the Rialto Theatre in 1920, establishing his presence in the San Antonio market. Eventually Santikos Theatres had a monopoly on the city that lasted until the late 1980s.

First Mall — Wonderland Mall, located on Fredricksburg Road on the outskirts of San Antonio, was the city's first mall, opening in 1960. The city grew, eventually placing the facility at the Loop 410/Fredricksburg Rd. interchange. The mall has gone through various changes and is now referred to as The Crossroads of San Antonio.

First Totally Air-Conditioned Skyscraper — The Milam Building downtown at the corner of Soledad and Travis was not only the city's first totally air-conditioned skyscraper, but the world's first. When it opened in 1928, San Antonians could not comprehend how air-conditioning would change the South.

First Hotel With Air-Conditioning — The St. Anthony Hotel is a landmark hotel in San Antonio. The hotel has sat across from Travis Park since 1909, playing host to presidents and celebrities. It is responsible for many innovations in the hotel industry. It is the first hotel in the world to offer air-conditioning, the first to have automatic doors, and the first to offer a drive-in registration desk.

First First-Class Hotel — The Hotel Menger, as it was originally named, was opened on February 2, 1859, in its present location on Alamo Plaza. The original building has been added on to several times. William Menger originally operated a brewery and decided to open a hotel to serve his patrons.

First Fiesta Event — The Battle of Flowers Parade is the oldest Fiesta event; it is a tradition which started in 1891. The event was originally scheduled for April 21 of that year but was rained out and postponed until the 24th (see First Battle of Flowers Parade).

First NIOSA — The first Night In Old San Antonio was held in 1938, and originally it was called the Indian Festival. The one-day event was patterned after early San Antonio fiestas. After a break during the second World War, the event was retitled the "River Carnival" in 1946. The name was changed to a Night In Old San Antonio in 1948, when the city asked the sponsoring organization, the Conservation Society, to move the event to Fiesta Week. In 1954 the event added a second day, and in 1958 it expanded to four days.

SECTION VIII
SAN ANTONIO LISTS

San Antonio Lists

Eight Structures That Have Been Moved From Their
Original Site To New Locations.

1. The Fairmount Hotel

Originally at the location of the Marriott Rivercenter, this building was moved to make way for the new downtown shopping center. The hotel is the largest building ever moved on pneumatic tires through municipal streets. It took weeks of preparation to ready the building for the move. Emmert International of Portland, Oregon, was hired to transport the structure. Thirty-six dollies, each with eight wheels, supported thirty steel beams, which in turn supported the hotel. The entire building was wrapped in steel cables.

The now-mobile hotel weighed in at 1,600 tons. There was great concern that the structure would cause damage to the Market Street bridge over the River Walk. The river had to be drained at that location, and extra supports were added to the bridge. On March 30, 1985, the Fairmount was ready to roll. The building was blessed by Auxiliary Bishop Bernard Popp before it left its resting place at Bowie and Commerce. It took six days before the building reached its new home at the corner of South Alamo and Nueva.

Thousands gathered to watch the hotel make its historic journey. True to the city's reputation, San Antonians made the event something of a party for onlookers. Vendors sold food, drinks, and souvenirs to the masses. The building moved at a snail's pace. It took four hours to turn a corner, and on the straightaways, it would reach a top speed of four miles an hour. The engineers found their first success when the building passed safely over the Market Street bridge. There were rumors circulating that Las Vegas had placed 7-1 odds against success, but gambling authorities dismissed this, saying the event was too weird to bet on.

As the hotel passed the Samuel Gompers statue on Market Street, many in the crowd rooted for the structure to knock over the disliked monument. (See "San Antonio's Six Most Unusual Historic Institutions" at the back of this book for the story.)

On April 4, 1985, the Fairmount reached its destination. The seventy-nine-year-old hotel, which had been abandoned for the last few years, had been saved. The building was set on a new foundation and refurbished into a first-class hotel.

2. The Original Alamo National Bank Building

This building on Commerce and Soledad was moved fifteen feet, in 1915, to accommodate the widening of Commerce Street. The widening of the street was privately financed, and the building was moved without even interrupting banking services.

3. The Playland Park Chapel

Also known as the Pleasant Valley Church, this small structure located near the Playland Park roller coaster was moved, in February 1987, to its new location at Anacacho and St. Gertrudis streets near O'Conner Road, where it has been renovated to become St. Edward's Anglican Catholic Church. The parish wanted to renovate the old chapel because it reminded them of an old English country chapel.

The chapel was built in 1964 atop one of the last sections of the Acequia Madre. It had been hidden in a corner of the park near the roller coaster and was dedicated to "everyone seeking a moment of peaceful meditation in this mixed-up world." Every half hour a recording of the Sermon on the Mount, recited by Melvin T. Munn, would play. The chapel sat vacant and deteriorated for seven years after Playland Park closed in 1980. The new congregation added stained glass windows, a new steeple, and a new altar when the building reached its new destination.

4. The Playland Park Roller Coaster

The Playland Rocket opened in 1941 and was once the largest roller coaster in South Texas. But when Playland Park closed in 1980, the screams of delighted riders were silenced. In January of 1985, Knoebel's Grove Amusement Park, in Elysburg, Pennsylvania, purchased the ride and moved it to its new location.

Over $750,000 was spent to move and restore the Rocket, which was cheaper than purchasing a new roller coaster. It took almost three months to disassemble and number each piece of wood, before shipping it all to Pennsylvania. The Rocket, which once was ranked as one of the ten best roller coasters, was reborn in the summer of 1985.

5. The O. Henry House

The former home of William Sydney Porter, or O. Henry as he was better known, was originally located at 904 South Presa. In 1959 its owner sold the adobe house to the San Antonio Conservation Society for one dollar, with the stipulation that the house be saved and moved to a new location. Many sites were investigated, and finally the Lone Star Brewery was chosen. The house was sold to Lone Star for one dollar in 1960 and is now part of their museum.

6. The August C. Stuemke Barn

This structure, originally located at 215 North Flores Street, was constructed in 1867 by August Struemke. The two-story building was given to the San Antonio Conservation Society by Frost National Bank, along with the funds to relocate it, in 1982. Master stonemason Curtis Smith dismantled the barn and meticulously numbered and photographed every stone for the reconstruction at its new location, 107 King William Street. The building is now used as a meeting place for the society.

7. Daniel Sullivan Stable and Coach House

This structure, designed by Alfred Giles, sat for many years in the parking lot of the *San Antonio Light's* building on Broadway and 4th. Built in 1896, the building once stood behind one of the stately mansions that used to grace

Broadway. In 1988 the coach house was moved to the Botanical Gardens.

8. The John Twohig House

John Twohig was known as the Breadline Banker of St. Mary's Street for his practice of handing out bread every Saturday night to the city's poor. Twohig was a banker and a merchant, who was best known for blowing up his store on Main Plaza, in 1842, to keep his stock of gun powder from falling into the hands of Mexican invaders.

Twohig's house was moved, brick by brick, from its location on St. Mary's Street downtown to a new home at the Witte Museum, in 1941. The Witte Museum also has the Francisco Ruiz house, moved from the south side of Military Plaza in 1942. Believed to have been built in 1765, it was once the home of a signer of the Declaration of Texas Independence.

Texas' Five Biggest Cities in 1900

1. San Antonio: population 53,300
2. Houston: 44,600
3. Dallas: 42,600
4. Galveston: 37,800
5. Fort Worth: 26,700

Six San Antonio Landmarks
That Are Built in Old Rock Quarries

1. Sunken Gardens and Sunken Garden Theatre

From 1880 to 1907 this area was the site of the Alamo Portland Cement Company. Operated by Englishman William Loyd, it was the first Portland Cement plant west of the Mississippi. Cement from the quarry was used in building the state capitol. When the plant was moved to Alamo Heights in 1907, the abandoned quarry was donated to the city.

It sat unused for ten years, but, thanks to a dream by Park Commissioner Ray Lambert, the scarred cavity came alive with flowers, a pagoda, walkways, and a lagoon. The old smokestack and kilns of the Portland Cement Company were incorporated into the design of the garden. Prisoners from the city jail were used to build the gardens and keep the cost down.

Originally, the name Japanese Sunken Gardens was given to the new facility. A Japanese couple maintained a tearoom there, but during World War II, with rising resentment toward the Japanese, the gardens were renamed the Chinese Sunken Gardens. One of the old entrances to the park still bears this name. Later the name was shortened to Sunken Gardens, until 1984, when the original name was restored.

2. Trinity University

Trinity University moved to San Antonio in 1942, from Waxahachie, Texas, and originally occupied the grounds of the San Antonio Female College (later Westmoreland College and The University of San Antonio), located on the northwest side of the city. After ten years, Trinity moved to the present site off U.S. 281 and Hildebrand Road. The virtually worthless piece of land has been transformed into one of the nation's most attractive campuses, thanks to the work of architects Bartlett Cocke and O'Neil Ford.

3. Alamo Stadium

Alamo Stadium was one of the city's greatest bargains. It was built in 1940 with $370,000 from the Depression-era WPA and with an additional $100,000 from the San Antonio School District. The original plan included a baseball field at one end of the grandstands, making the stadium a multipurpose "L"-shaped facility.

The field was dedicated on September 20, 1940, in an area of town that was without much development. The governor was on hand for the festivities, and the first event was a doubleheader football game. In game one, Corpus Christi High beat Jefferson 14-0. In the second contest, Brackenridge outdueled Houston Reagan 19-2. The stadium was an instant success. Its bowl shape, lighted field, and spacious press box made it an extremely modern facility. It made enough money in eight years to pay off the bonds used for its construction. In 1950 Alamo Gym was built with the profits from the stadium. (Alamo Gym, known for many years as a sweatbox, was not air conditioned until 1989.)

Alamo Stadium was one of many names under consideration for the facility. A city-wide poll conducted by a local paper showed that "The Chili Bowl" was most popular with local students. Other suggestions included Bexar Bowl, Blue Bonnet Field, Cactus Field, Huisache Bowl (named after the street), Laurel Field (after the neighborhood), Mission Stadium, San Antonio Stadium, and Hollers Field (in honor of the school board president).

4. The San Antonio Zoo

Located in Brackenridge Park, the San Antonio Zoo is one of the best zoos in Texas. The Spaniards got stone for their homes in these ancient quarries, and the water that runs through the zoo is from an ancient acequia. The old quarries have been recrafted into numerous "barless cages," which were some of the first in the United States.

The animal collection at the zoo is excellent. It has one of the world's largest collections of antelopes and cranes (including the whooping crane, of which there are less than 1000 in the world). Many exotic animals were first bred in the U.S. at the San Antonio Zoo. They include the American flamingo, the white rhinoceros, and the dama gazelle.

The San Antonio Zoo has also become an innovator in fund-raising. Each April Fool's Day, the zoo would be besieged with calls from unsuspecting victims of practical jokers returning calls for Mr. C. Lyon or Mrs. G. Raffe. In the mid-1980s, the Zoological Society decided to make the best of a bad situation and have volunteers man the switchboard throughout the day. Now, when somebody calls and asks to speak to Mr. L. E. Phant, the person is informed that he has been a victim of an April Fool's gag and is then asked to make a donation to the zoo. The program has become so successful that other zoos across the country have started similar programs.

5. Lincoln Heights Subdivision in Alamo Heights
This was the second site of the Alamo Portland Cement Company. The company moved to Alamo Heights in 1907, when it outgrew its old site. When this plant was built, it was still three miles from the end of the streetcar line and pretty much a wild, untamed piece of land. The company built its own little town on the site called Cementville, complete with school, church, company store, and small frame houses. When the company moved all of its operation to Loop 1604 and Green Mountain Road in 1985, the company town died, and the site was shut down and sold to developers.

6. Fiesta Texas
Work is now being completed for an amusement park, golf course, and an office and retail development center to be built in a quarry located on the north side of the city near 1604 and I-10. The amusement park is being designed by the folks who built Opryland in Nashville. This park will showcase Texas and its music.

Seven Military Leaders Who Have
Spent Time in San Antonio

1. Theodore Roosevelt
Roosevelt was the assistant secretary of the Navy when he first thought to form a cavalry regiment of wild West-types to fight the Spaniards in Cuba. The "Rough Riders" ended up being a mix of westerners and East Coast Ivy Leaguers. Some of the frontiersman included "Rocky Mountain Bill," "Rattlesnake Pete," "Lariat Ned," and "Broncho George," a man who had already downed five men. The westerners drew less attention than the nattily dressed, refined East Coast college educated men, who stood out in roughshod San Antonio.

Contrary to popular belief, Roosevelt was not the commanding officer of the Rough Riders. Feeling that he lacked enough military experience, the assistant secretary chose Colonel Leonard Wood, who had seen action in the Indian campaigns, as the head man. Roosevelt became a lieutenant

Teddy Roosevelt while training with the Rough Riders in San Antonio.

colonel under Wood. Roosevelt arrived on May 15, 1898, and recruited members for his crew from the lobby of the Menger Hotel. The bar at the hotel was the site of many impassioned speeches by the future president. The Menger Bar is still intact and has been renamed the Roosevelt Bar.

The First United States Volunteer Cavalry trained on the site of Riverside Golf Course, near the water hazard on the sixteenth hole. On May 30, 1898, the volunteer cavalry left by train for Florida, then they went on to Cuba. The Rough Riders suffered many casualties, due to both war and disease. After three months, the Rough Riders were disbanded. Lt. Colonel Roosevelt went on to bigger and better endeavors.

2. Dwight D. Eisenhower

The future president first came to San Antonio's Fort Sam Houston in 1915, after graduating from the U.S. Military Academy. Eisenhower's two-year stay in San Antonio would change his life forever. It was here that he met Mamie Doud. The young socialite was from Denver, but she spent her winters in San Antonio with her family. While in town, Mamie attended Mulholland School (which later merged with St. Mary's Hall). Dwight wanted to become a member of the Army's Signal Corps, where he could become one of the Army's early aviators, but concerns from the Doud family made him rethink his career path. After a whirlwind romance, the two decided to marry. The lieutenant bought a ring for $70 from Hertzberg Jewelers, and the couple soon moved into Eisenhower's cramped two-room Bachelor Officer's Quarters.

The apartment on the corner of Grayson and New Braunfels, which still stands today, was known as Club Eisenhower for the number of parties the young couple hosted for their contemporaries. While in San Antonio, Dwight also spent time coaching the Peacock Military Academy football team in 1915 and the St. Mary's football team in 1916.

Eisenhower returned to San Antonio in 1941. This time he and Mamie lived on the corner of Dickman and New Braunfels in a house that is now known as the Eisenhower Quarters. The newly promoted general came to San Antonio as the new chief of staff for the Third Army. Because of a building shortage on the post, Eisenhower's offices were downtown in the Tower Life Building. The Third Army occupied the sixth and seventh floor, and the general had his office in the corner on the seventh floor. His stay in San Antonio was short lived; after Pearl Harbor was attacked, the general was reassigned.

3. Douglas MacArthur

MacArthur lived in San Antonio when his father was the commander at Fort Sam Houston. The main parade field at the post is named for his father, Arthur MacArthur, and not Douglas. The young MacArthur studied at West Texas Military Academy, which was located across from the army post. (The school eventually merged with Texas Military Institute and San Antonio Academy.)

MacArthur graduated in 1897 at the top of his class, with a 97.35 average. He was captain of the football team and a champion orator. After a five-year stay in the city he went on to West Point.

MacArthur was stationed at Fort Sam Houston in 1911 and was a captain of the engineers.

4. Black Jack Pershing

The Commanding General's Quarters on Fort Sam are named in honor of John Pershing, who lived there in 1917. Pershing spent time here and on the Mexican border in skirmishes with Pancho Villa. When World War I broke out, Pershing left Fort Sam Houston to command U.S. forces.

Pershing was not originally called on to take on Villa. The task was originally given to General Frederick Funston (for whom Funston Loop is named). Funston died unexpectedly at a function at the St. Anthony Hotel in 1917. Funston was given the rare honor of having his body lie in state at the Alamo. His command was handed to Pershing.

5. Robert E. Lee

Stationed in San Antonio in the late 1850s, Lee was commander of the local troops from February to December of 1860, in the days before Fort Sam Houston. The then-lieutenant colonel was a popular member of local society and often frequented the German Casino Club.

He was also the first Life member of the St. Mark's Diocesan Missionary Society and laid the cornerstone at St. Mark's Episcopal Church.

Lee was in San Antonio when he made his historic decision to commit his allegiances to Virginia in the War between the States. On February 16, 1861, Lee met with secessionists who told him to resign his commission and join them, otherwise he was to leave for Washington without his belongings. Lee charged that he was loyal to the Union and to Virginia, not to Texas revolutionaries. Lee left Texas without his property, and though he asked for them several times, he never saw his belongings, or Texas, again.

6. Charles Lindbergh

Lindbergh flew his own private plane to Stinson Field on March 24, 1924, and entered the Army as a cadet at Brooks Field. One hundred and four would-be aviators started training on Jenny aircraft. By September only thirty-four cadets remained as advanced training shifted to Kelly Field. The class trained on the more powerful De Havilland aircraft.

Nine days before graduation, Lindbergh had an accident and had to bail out of his aircraft. Luckily for him, he was a member of the first class of cadets who trained with a new-fangled invention called the parachute. Lucky Lindy was only the twelfth military person ever to use his parachute.

On March 25, 1925, he graduated from the top of his class and accepted a second lieutenant commission and an assignment in the Reserve Corps.

A park named for the famed aviator is located on Kelly Air Force Base.

7. Edward White

Edward White, the first American to walk in space, was a San Antonio native, born on November 14, 1930, when his father was stationed at Fort Sam Houston. White was a member of the Gemini 4 mission when he walked in space for twenty-two minutes on June 3, 1965. After the successful mission, the city threw a parade in his honor on June 16 of that year.

Colonel White was killed January 27, 1967, along with Gus Grissom and Roger Chaffee, when the capsule of Apollo 1 caught on fire.

Other military leaders who have spent time in San Antonio include aviation pioneers Billy Mitchell, Hap Arnold, Jimmy Doolittle, Claire Channault, and Frank M. Hawk. General Joseph W. "Vinegar Joe" Stillwell, who commanded U.S. troops in Burma during World War II, also served in San Antonio.

San Antonio's Ten Most Influential Architects

In November of 1989, *Texas Architecture* magazine included the following (with the exception of Alfred Giles) as nine of Texas' most influential architects.

1. O'Neil Ford

O'Neil Ford's mark has been left on every corner of the city. Perhaps the city's most famous designer, Ford never had the benefit of a formal education. With only two years of undergraduate work at North Texas Teachers College (now the University of North Texas) and a basic architecture course from the International Correspondence School of Scranton, Pennsylvania, he entered the office of Dallas architect David R. Williams as an apprentice. Williams served as his first role model, and together they designed homes throughout Texas.

When Williams was appointed administrator of the National Youth Administration in 1936, he was able to direct commissions to Ford, the first being the Little Chapel of the Woods on the campus of Texas Women's University in Denton. The young designer came to San Antonio as a consulting designer in the restoration of La Villita, another NYA project.

Over the years, Ford has designed some of the city's biggest projects, including portions of Trinity University, the first phase of UTSA, and the Tower of the Americas. Ford also designed a plan for Hemisfair Plaza that would have incorporated more of the historic buildings into the Fair site, but it was rejected.

Ford was appointed to the National Council of the Arts in 1968 by Lyndon Johnson and to the American Council for Arts in Education in 1975 by David Rockefeller. The first endowed chair in the School of Architecture at the University of Texas was named for Ford. A small plaza in La Villita behind the Little Church was also named in honor of the architect. O'Neil Ford died in 1982.

2. Atlee B. and Robert M. Ayres

Atlee Ayres founded his firm in the late 1890s and was joined by his son in 1924. Together they designed some of San Antonio's most impressive projects, including the city's first skyscraper, the Smith-Young Tower (now the Tower Life Building), along with the Federal Reserve (now the Mexican Consulate), and the Plaza Hotel (now Granada Homes). This total project, built right before the Depression, was one of the biggest undertakings of its time. Its owner wanted the complex on the corner of Villita and St. Mary's to be the new center of downtown.

Another structure designed by the pair was the City Central Bank and Trust Building (now the South Texas Building) on the corner of Navarro and Houston. When it was constructed in 1919, it was the costliest bank building in Texas and the tallest in the city—thus its nickname, "The Million Dollar Bank." The YWCA (now the Blood Bank) and the old City Public Service Building were also of their design.

Ayres and Ayres were also responsible for the administration building on Randolph Air Force Base, better known as Taj Mahal, and the Municipal Auditorium. They also designed the Atkinson home, which is now the McNay Art Institute.

An office building at the corner of Travis and Broadway is named for Atlee Ayres. The structure was built in 1911 and renamed on April 17, 1985, in honor of its architect, who had his offices there until 1928. Ayres also designed the adjacent Moore building (now 110 Broadway) and was also the state architect of Texas in 1915. The firm of Ayres and Ayres was always kept small. It closed in 1977, at the death of son Robert Ayres.

3. Alfred Giles

Born in England, Alfres Giles chose San Antonio as his home in 1873. He designed courthouse buildings throughout South Texas and numerous buildings in San Antonio. Giles left his mark on San Antonio, even though he commenced work in the city over 100 years ago.

Some of the city's most prominent structures owe their existence to Giles. They include the Bexar County Courthouse, the Fort Sam Infantry Post barracks, the Mother House at Incarnate Word College, the Menger Hotel, the Crockett building on Alamo Plaza, and the old Bexar County Jail on Cameron Street. Like many prominent architects, Giles began by designing homes. He built many of the mansions in the King William District, including the Steves home and the Groos home. His firm also drew up the plans for the Terrell Castle and the commander's house at Fort Sam Houston.

Many of his architectural gems have been lost over the years, such as Haymarket Plaza, the original Joske's Brothers store, the original Groos Bank, and the first Brackenridge High School. Luckily, a majority of his work has been saved and renovated in San Antonio, and very few South Texas counties are without a Giles courthouse.

4. Carlton Adams

Adams, along with his uncle Carl C. Adams, operated the city's leading commercial architecture firm from the 1910s to the 1950s. Adams' most famous work was Jefferson High School, which received national attention in *Life* magazine in 1937 as the "most outstanding modern school in the U.S." Adams was also responsible for the design of the Alamo Cenotaph, which featured sculptures by Pompeo Copini.

The San Antonio Drug Company's offices on the corner of St. Mary's and Market, along with the Great American Life Insurance Building (1925) and the National Bank of Commerce (1925), were projects of Adams' firm. Perhaps his most prestigious work was the Hall of State in Dallas Fair Park for the Texas Centennial in 1936. Adams also designed the Student Union at Texas A&M and monkey island at the San Antonio Zoo.

5. Ralph Cameron

Cameron began working as a draftsman for Alfred Giles at age thirteen and later worked for Adams & Adams in 1912. He opened his own office in 1914, and he was appointed the architect of the San Antonio School Board in 1915.

Cameron's best works are within blocks of each other. He was the supervising architect of the Scottish Rite Temple in 1924. He also collaborated on the post office and U.S. courthouse on Alamo Plaza. The Medical Arts Building (now the Alamo Plaza Hotel) across the street was also his design.

The architect was responsible for several homes in Monte Vista and Olmos Park, including the Hornaday house and the Spencer residence.

6. Robert Hugman

A San Antonio native, Robert Hugman had a vision that became one of the strongest forces ever in San Antonio, the River Walk. Hugman was the architect who envisioned the Paseo Del Rio as it is today. However, in the late 1920s, such a plan was not popular. Many wanted simply to pave over the river to prevent flooding. But Hugman envisioned a developed river walk known as "The Shops of Aragon and Romula." Because of a fight with city hall, Hugman was relieved of his duties as the project's architect right before its completion. Hugman finished his career as an employee of Randolph Air Force Base. He took great pride in the development of the River Walk, especially after Hemisfair, when his vision grew into reality. The bells at Arneson River Theatre were dedicated on November 1, 1978, in honor of his service to the city.

7. Bartlett Cocke

Cocke returned to his hometown of San Antonio in 1924, after graduating from M.I.T.'s School of Architecture. He began as an apprentice for the Kelwood Company and opened his own office in 1927. During the Depression, he was the deputy director of the Historical American Building Survey, producing drawings of several pre-Civil War Texas structures.

His first major project came in 1938, when he beat out Ralph Cameron and Ayres & Ayres to design the Joske's building (now Rivercenter) for Alamo Plaza. Cocke traveled across the country, visiting fifty-seven department stores before drawing up the plans for the critically acclaimed Joske's building. After his success, Cocke went on to design many office buildings, malls, and public schools, including a joint venture with O'Neil Ford to build Trinity University and UTSA.

Bartlett Cocke has also become the first University of Texas alumni to be honored with a professorship in his name. He also served as the president of the Texas Society of Architects in 1944-1945.

8. George Wills

Wills arrived in San Antonio in 1910, at the age of 31. He was one of the most studied architects in Texas at the time, working as a draftsman for Frank Lloyd Wright, then with a number of prairie school practitioners. When he first arrived in the city, he worked for Ayres & Ayres, before opening his own firm in 1917.

Wills' Milam Building in 1928 was the tallest reinforced concrete building in the world—and the first to be air-conditioned. His designs include the addition to the Bexar County Courthouse, the Sunken Garden Theatre, and he worked with Emmett T. Jackson and Ayres & Ayres to build the Municipal Auditorium.

9. Henry J. Steinbomer

A man of strong faith, Steinbomer was Texas' premier church architect in the 1940s and 1950s. He co-founded the Historic Buildings Foundation and worked with sculptor Gutzon Borglum and Clara Driscoll in persuading the city to preserve the Alamo. He also worked with Bartlett Cocke and

Fred Buenz to save several historic homes now on the grounds of the Witte Museum.

Steinbomer's first church project was an education building for Alamo Heights Methodist Church. He later planned the chapel and several additions to the grounds. Between World War II and 1964, he designed over seventy-five church projects in San Antonio and over 150 in South Texas, including the Travis Park Methodist Youth Building, St. Luke's Episcopal Church, and Jefferson Methodist Church.

10. Andrew Perez III
Perez is a former disciple of O'Neil Ford, working with him from 1966 to 1970. He has designed several houses, schools, banks, and office buildings throughout South Texas. His most noted work came in 1982, during the battle over the Texas Theatre, when appointed by Mayor Cisneros to head a task force on historic preservation. The committee registered over a thousand historic buildings and wrote a nationally acclaimed historic preservation ordinance that was adopted by the city council in 1987.

In 1987 Perez took over as the head of the School of Architecture at UTSA, where he is working to win accreditation for the school.

Six Places in San Antonio That Are Replicas

1. The Roosevelt Bar
This bar in the Menger Hotel is a replica of the bar in the House of Lords in London. Only this one is located on Alamo Plaza and is open to the public. The Menger family sent an architect to London to copy the bar. It was built in 1881, at a cost of $60,000. Originally named the Menger Bar, it was later redubbed the Roosevelt Bar after Teddy Roosevelt recruited his Rough Riders there.

2. Lourdes Grotto Sanctuary
This sanctuary is an exact replica of the Shrine of Lourdes in southern France. The sanctuary is located on the grounds of the Oblate Seminary, at 285 Oblate Drive.

3. San Pedro Playhouse

Located in San Pedro Park and home to San Antonio's Little Theatre, the front of this building is a replica of the old Market House located on Market Street in the 1850s.

4. Shrine of the Little Flower

This westside church, on the corner of Zarzamora and Kentucky, was built in 1931, and it is a replica of a church in France. The parish is a memorial to Sister Therese, a cloistered Carmelite nun, who was known as the Little Flower. The church cost over a half million dollars to construct and contributions came from around the world.

The altar statues are from Spain and the stations of the cross were cast in Germany. The altar is made of Carrara marble. The names of those who donated money for the shrine are engraved in marble inside the church.

5. Pizza Hut/Billy Reuter's Saloon

Located across from the Alamo is perhaps the nicest Pizza Hut ever to slice pepperoni. The restaurant is located in the building which once housed Billy Reuter's Saloon. The saloon was once a favorite of patrons of the Grand Opera House located on the opposite corner. Theatre-goers would visit the bar during intermission, and the saloon would ring a bell when the second act was about to begin.

When the bar closed, the space was occupied by Hutchins Co. (a men's clothing store) and later by a women's store. In 1986 Pizza Hut renovated the old retail space into a replica of the old saloon. A forty-foot bar and tile floor are reminiscent of the originals. The tin ceilings and the cast iron columns are left over from the old saloon. The Pizza Hut has added murals to the walls and has been faithful to the historic motif.

6. The White House

On the north side of San Antonio, just inside the loop, is a private residence that is a replica of the White House. Because it is a private residence, the author has chosen not to pass along the address—you will have to find it yourself.

San Antonio's Six Most Unusual Historic Institutions

1. The Samuel Gompers Statue

Probably the most disliked statue in the city, the Gompers monument rests on Market Street across from the convention center. During the moving of the Fairmount Hotel down Market Street in 1985, onlookers were rooting for the building to run into the statue.

Gompers established the American Federation of Labor in 1886. The AFL started with 150,000 highly skilled craftsmen, who were not easily replaced by strike breakers. Therefore, the union was extremely successful in gaining concessions from employers. The labor movement was mainly on the East Coast and had little effect on San Antonio, which was beyond the reach of the industrial revolution and early labor activity at the time.

The only reason the statue of Gompers sits in downtown is that he had the misfortune of dying in San Antonio, at the St. Anthony Hotel in 1924, as his train was stopping over in the city after attending an international labor conference in Mexico. The monument was given to the city by the AFL-CIO in 1974.

2. The Pat Memorial

Located on Wilson Avenue on Fort Sam Houston, this memorial was erected in honor of Pat the Horse, who retired after twenty-six years of military service when the 12th Field Artillery Unit was motorized. Pat died in 1953, at the age of forty-six, but his memory lives on.

3. The Water Museum

Established in 1976 in a historic home on the City Water Board property, the Water Museum is the only one in existence in the world. The old home on Commerce Street is run by the water board, but has irregular hours and is such a well-kept secret, that many water board employees have no knowledge of its existence.

4. The Shrine of Our Lady of Czestochowa

Located at 138 Beethoven Street on the east side, this shrine commemorates 1000 years of Polish Christianity. Built in 1966, it honors the black Madonna, Poland's most important religious icon. In addition, the pink granite memorial also honors silent film star Pola Negri, who made San Antonio her home in the twilight of her life. It is the only shrine anywhere that honors both.

Nuns from Poland staff the facility, and masses in Polish are held daily.

5. The North Pole Marker

Ever wonder how many miles to the North Pole? Someone obviously did. At the southeast corner of Dewey and Main, behind San Antonio College, sits a marker that points out that the North Pole is 4,189 miles away. The building on which the marker sits has passed through many hands, and no one seems to know why the sign is there.

6. The Old Ursuline Academy's Three-Sided Clock Tower

When the old convent and school were built on Convent Street, it was on the edge of town. Since no one lived to the north of the academy, the tower was built without a clock facing that direction. The young ladies who attended the academy used to say that there was no clock on the north side because they would not be caught giving the time of day to a Yankee.

Fourteen Terms That Every
San Antonian Should Know

1. NIOSA

An acronym that stands for "Night in Old San Antonio." This annual Fiesta event, held in La Villita and sponsored by the Conservation Society, is the highlight of the ten-day celebration.

2. 09 (pronounced oh-nine)

A slang term for the city of Alamo Heights. The term is derived from the last two digits in the area's zip code, 78209.

If someone was referred to as an 09er, that would mean they were from Alamo Heights.

3. Inky Word

A nickname given to the Catholic girls' high school, Incarnate Word, located on Hildebrand, off 281. (e.g., Buffy is an Inky Word girl and an 09er.)

4. Icehouse

Many lifelong San Antonians refer to convenience stores as icehouses. This is a throwback to the days when ice for home refrigerators was purchased at neighborhood icehouses. Some of these icehouses later began selling bread, milk, and beer, and they eventually evolved to the modern day convenience store. For many San Antonians, it is still a tradition to gather at a small neighborhood icehouse on a Friday afternoon and partake in an ice cold one.

5. Saint Joske's

Refers to Saint Joseph's Catholic Church. This downtown church is surrounded by the old Joske's building and was jokingly dubbed Saint Joske's. The Joske's building is now part of Rivercenter Mall, but Saint Rivercenter never caught on.

6. Gucci B

The nickname given to the upscale H.E.B. grocery store located in Alamo Heights (one of the few grocery stores in the world to have an elevator).

7. The Strip

The strip is a portion of St. Mary's Street near Trinity that features a variety of eclectic clubs and restaurants.

8. The Loop

Locals refer to Loop 410 simply as the loop. This has led to a variety of new phrases, such as loopland (generally refers to north San Antonio). The "loop" can also be used as a point of reference (i.e., Take Bandera Road, 2 miles north of the loop).

9. The Death Loop

Not to be confused with "the loop," the death loop refers to Loop 1604, which at one time had only two lanes and very few lights, on the heavily traveled north side. Because of the high number of accidents on the roadway, it was given the gruesome moniker.

10. Taj Mahal

San Antonians refer to the combination water tower/administration offices/theatre at Randolph Air Force Base as Taj Mahal. The unique structure was designed by Robert B. Ayres and Atlee Ayres.

11. Henry B. and Henry C.

Refers to two politicians who changed the face of San Antonio. Henry B. is Congressman Henry B. Gonzales, the first Hispanic member of the U.S. Congress and the city's first Hispanic city councilman.

Henry C. is Henry Cisneros, the city's first Hispanic mayor and a symbol of San Antonio's growth and prosperity in the 1980s.

12. The Chili Bowl

The annual football game between the Indians of Harlandale High School and the Buffaloes of Fox Tech is dubbed the Chili Bowl.

13. Raspas

The famous and often controversial snowcones sold in front of the Alamo are most often referred to by the Spanish name, "raspas."

14. Fort Sam

Come on, nobody calls it Fort Sam Houston.

Five San Antonio Projects That Were
Conceived But Never Became Reality

1. The Alamo Monument

In 1912 the Alamo Heroes Monument Association was chartered, with the goal to erect a monument in Alamo Plaza in honor of those who lost their lives in the battle. The A.H.M.A. supported a plan by architect Alfred Giles to build an 802-foot tower which would have cost two million dollars. The tower would be surrounded by thirty-foot-tall statues of Alamo heroes and would have four elevators to take sightseers to the top. Once at the top, you would be able to see for 100 miles. Near the ground level, the first stories would be filled with museums, galleries, and a library.

Because of the cost of the project and its dimensions (it would have dwarfed the Alamo and everything else in downtown), enthusiasm for the project diminished.

2. Boardwalk and Baseball

When Sea World of Texas was built, there were plans to build an adjacent amusement park dubbed Boardwalk and Baseball. The park was modeled after a similar park in Florida, also owned by Sea World's parent company, Harcourt, Brace and Jahanovich. Unlike Sea World, the new park would feature a variety of rides, including roller coasters and possibly a baseball stadium.

The project first became questionable when Opryland USA announced its intention to build a similar theme park in north San Antonio. Plans for Boardwalk and Baseball were quietly pushed further back when HB&J sold Sea World to Anheuser Busch.

3. A 60,000-Seat Alamo Stadium

When Clinton Manges was awarded the San Antonio franchise in the United States Football League, he announced his intention to expand the high school stadium to 60,000 seats by 1986. This would give the city a facility capable of hosting major league attractions and also meet conditions set by the new league. Manges backed up his promise by signing a 30-year lease backed up by two ten-year options.

Manges did give the stadium a new track, Astroturf field, and a fresh coat of paint in the team's colors, but that was the extent of the improvements. Unfortunately for the city, Manges could barely afford to pay his players, much less expand the stadium's capacity. The league and the team folded in 1986, leaving Alamo Stadium virtually unchanged.

4. A Downtown University of Texas at San Antonio Campus

After Hemisfair '68, many considered the ninety-two-acre tract an ideal place for the new university. The campus would have been centrally located, so that all would have equal access to the facility. It would also play an important role in the revitalization of downtown. However, the UT Board of Regents rejected downtown, in favor of donated land on the far north side. The land (donated by people who had vast land holdings in the area and would benefit from development) effectively made the new school a commuter campus.

As for the Hemisfair site, it sat vacant for many years, just a shell of its former self. Twenty years after the world fair, the fairgrounds were redeveloped into a park for 133 million dollars.

5. The Centennial Exposition

Competition for the Texas Centennial Exposition was fierce among the cities of Texas. San Antonio put in its own bid to host Texas' 100th anniversary by proposing to build a fairground on the city's east side near Freeman Coliseum. A street in the area was named Exposition Avenue in anticipation of the event.

The Exposition was eventually awarded to Dallas, which held the festivities at the State Fair site. As for Exposition Avenue, it was recently renamed Coca Cola Boulevard for the nearby bottling plant.

Seven Things That San Antonio Does Not Have

1. A University in the Southwest Conference

San Antonio is the only major city in Texas not to have a representative in the Southwest Conference. Dallas (SMU), Austin (UT), and Fort Worth (TCU) all are accounted for, and Houston has two schools (Rice and Houston). Even Waco (Baylor), Lubbock (Texas Tech), and College Station (Texas A & M) are invited to the party.

2. A Reservoir

San Antonio is one of the largest cities in the world to rely solely on an underground water supply, the Edwards Aquifer. The pureness of the water in the massive underground lake made water relatively cheap because treatment plants were not necessary. The city had an abundant supply of some of the cleanest water in the world.

But new demands put on the aquifer because of the city's massive growth have forced the city to investigate various reservoir proposals.

3. Fluoridated Water

San Antonio is the largest city in America to have a water supply free of fluoride. Despite efforts from the medical community in 1985, the general public has always voted to keep the dental aid out of the city's drinking water.

4. A Locally Owned Department Store

Like every other major American city, San Antonio once had its share of locally owned department stores. Joske's, Frost Brothers, and Wolff & Marx were a major part of the local retail scene; however, by 1990 they all had vanished.

5. Loop 410/Highway 281 Interchange

When the San Antonio city fathers decided that the city needed a freeway to reach the north side, they never imagined the controversy that would ensue. Just about everybody agreed that such a freeway was needed, but nobody could agree on the exact location. Some wanted it to follow San Pedro, others wanted it to assume the course of

Broadway, while some thought the rail tracks that passed through Olmos Park Golf Course would be the best path.

When the city finally decided on the route, the fight really began. Citizens of Olmos Park thought it was too close to their enclave. Zoo officials were upset that it cut off a buffalo pasture (which highway officials claim was just a dumping ground). The federal government chose not to sponsor the project because it went through park land (the highway was to be I-37 rather than U.S. 281). The highway department also had problems securing land for a 410/281 interchange. Despite a costly court battle, private citizens were able to hold onto the land slated for the on-ramps. Thus, two of San Antonio's biggest freeways were built without a way for motorists to conveniently exit from one freeway to the other.

6. A College Bowl Game

San Antonio is the only major city in Texas not to have hosted a postseason college bowl game in the last forty years. Houston had the Bluebonnet Bowl and Dallas hosts the Cotton Bowl. Even El Paso, a city a fraction of the size of San Antonio, hosts the John Hancock Bowl (formerly the Sun Bowl).

The city was the host of the Alamo Bowl game in 1947, but it was not successful and the event lasted only one year. With the soon-to-be-constructed Alamodome, area sports boosters are hoping that this will soon change.

7. A Downtown Grocery Store

When H.L. Green's on Alamo Plaza closed in the mid-1980s, so did the city's last downtown grocery store. Advocates for the city's core felt that a food outlet was still needed for the many people who live downtown, and for the many more who were looking forward to new downtown housing projects. A couple of convenience outlets have since opened, but the area is still in desperate need of a full-service grocery store.

Ten Facts About San Fernando Cathedral

San Fernando Cathedral is located on Main Avenue across from Main Plaza. It is the cathedral for the San Antonio Catholic Diocese and has become, in addition to a place of worship, a local tourist attraction.

1. The cornerstone for the church was placed in 1738, although construction was not started for three years. The church is older than the United States, and it is the oldest cathedral in the United States.

2. After the missions became secularized in 1794, San Fernando became the warehouse for mission properties. Today, the church archives contain priceless records and documents from all the missions.

The city's last streetcar on its final day of service, April 29, 1933, in front of San Fernando Cathedral.

3. Alamo defender James Bowie was married there on April 25, 1831, to Miss Ursula de Vermendi. The ceremony was performed by Don Refugio de la Garza.

4. Colonel William Travis, on the days preceding the Battle of the Alamo, used the church's tower as a lookout.

5. The church has at one time or another been partially destroyed by war, flood, and fire. It has always been rebuilt.

6. From 1868 until 1890, the cathedral had only one tower, the north one, giving it a lopsided look.

7. In 1902 the Claretian Fathers were given their first assignment in the United States at San Fernando. The church was the beginning of all their activities in this country.

8. San Fernando once had its own school on South Laredo Street. The school was built in 1930, and the gym, in 1948. The city took control of the buildings in 1967.

9. In 1970, amidst much controversy, the Romanesque towers were removed from the cathedral which restored San Fernando to its original design. Some felt the removal was a bad idea, because it lessened the dramatic impact of the church. Others approved because it fell in line with the historical design of the building.

10. At one time, the dome on the cathedral was an important benchmark for map makers. The landmark was considered the center of San Antonio, and all streets would be designated north, south, east, or west by their relationship to the dome. (That has been changed; Commerce and Main are now the indicating streets.) For many years, the dome was also the mark for which all distances to San Antonio were measured.

Eleven Facts About the Menger Hotel

Located on Alamo Plaza, the Menger Hotel is rich with history. Originally making the building a brewery, William Menger soon saw the need for a first-class hotel in the Alamo City. Opening over 100 years ago on February 2, 1859, the Menger Hotel gave San Antonio the first "first-class" hotel west of the Mississippi. The following are some of the unusual footnotes in the Menger's history.

1. The Roosevelt Bar is an exact replica of the one in the House of Lords in London. The bar was once in the front of the hotel, then later was moved to a newer part of the hotel on Crockett Street. There are now plans to move the bar to Blum Street. The photos on the wall of the bar depict San Antonio in its early days.

2. The Roosevelt Bar is named for Teddy Roosevelt, who recruited his Rough Riders in the hotel bar and lobby. Officially known as the First U.S. Volunteer Calvary, the Rough Riders were organized in 1898 and trained in south San Antonio in the area now occupied by Roosevelt Park and Riverside Golf Course.

The Menger Hotel overlooking Alamo Plaza.

In 1905 President Roosevelt and his men returned to San Antonio for a reunion at the Menger.

3. The hotel guest list has included presidents Teddy Roosevelt, Taft, McKinley, Lyndon Johnson, Reagan, Truman, Eisenhower, and Nixon; film stars John Wayne, Joan Crawford, James Stewart, Robert Mitchum, Bob Hope, Jose Ferrer, Sarah Bernhardt; and army generals Grant and Lee.

4. The Menger has served up many unusual foods, including turtles which were taken from the San Antonio River.

5. If you have ever seen Rock Hudson, James Dean, and Elizabeth Taylor in the film *Giant*, you may have noticed the large painting in Rock Hudson's den. The mammoth painting depicting a prairie scene was borrowed from the Menger. It hangs on the second floor of the original building.

6. The hotel's "King Suite" is named after the owners of the famous King Ranch. Captain Richard King died while staying at the Menger in 1865. The room has changed little since his death, with a four-poster canopy bed dominating the room.

Another suite received its name from famous guests. The Roy Rogers suite, decorated in rawhide and leather furnishings, once hosted Roy Rogers and Dale Evans during their movie-making days.

7. Mysterious tunnels occupy the ground underneath the original part of the hotel. The walls are two to three feet thick, and the tunnels once served as cold storage for the old brewery. It is rumored that one of the tunnels leads to the Alamo and was used as an escape route during the historic siege. This, of course, is ridiculous because the Menger was built twenty-three years after the fall. This rumor is most likely associated with the fact that one of the tunnels is part of the old Alamo Madre Ditch, an ancient acequia that once served the mission.

8. Stone for the original part of the hotel was taken from the rock quarry on the north side of town, which is now Sunken Gardens.

9. Poet Sydney Lanier wrote about San Antonio while boarding at the Menger. Writer O. Henry often mentioned the Menger in his many writings about San Antonio.

10. At one time, alligators were kept on the Menger's patio. The most famous was Old Bill Menger, who was given to the hotel by a guest who was unable to pay his bill. Old Bill lived for fifty years and had become quite endearing. Old Bill died in the 1930s when he got in a tussle with another patio gator.

11. In the 1940s the Menger almost became a parking lot. The hotel had fallen on hard times. It had lost a lot of its prestige and needed extensive repairs. Prospective buyers purchased an option on the downtown landmark in 1940 and announced that it would be razed. An outcry of support arose from across the country, and the option was passed. The hotel was later purchased by W. L. Moody of Galveston, who restored the building.

San Antonio's Eleven Favorite Ghost Stories

Every town has various tales of spirits that inhabit the area. San Antonio has its share. What follows are some of the city's most popular.

1. The Ghost Crossing — Perhaps the most popular tale, the ghost crossing, has enticed thousands of San Antonians to trek out to an obscure southeast railroad crossing to participate in an eerie phenomenon.

The ghost crossing is on Shane Road, where it intersects with the Southern Pacific rail line. According to the legend, a school bus full of kids stalled on the tracks and was hit by a train. Today, when a motorist stops his car before the tracks and places it in neutral, the ghosts of those children will push the car over the tracks.

To visit the crossing, take Presa south off S.E. Military Drive. Turn right on Southton Road, then right again on

Shane. Turn off your engine and give it a try. If you're brave, visit the crossing at night. You will be amazed when your car mysteriously moves across the tracks. Is it an optical illusion? Are you really moving downhill? Or is your car being pushed across by ghosts?

2. The Ghostly Nuns — The basement of Santa Rosa Hospital is said to be the haunting grounds for these spectral beings. The ghosts are believed to be the spirits of five nuns who died on October 30, 1912, after trying to rescue children from a burning orphanage. The wooden building of the St. John's Orphan Asylum, which went up in flames that night, was located across from the hospital at the corner of Houston and San Saba.

3. The Menger Ghost — Said to haunt the old portion of the Menger Hotel, this ghost is believed to be that of Sallie White, a former hotel chambermaid who was murdered by her husband years earlier. This poltergeist is rather stubborn, appearing only when she pleases.

4. The Alamo Ghosts — Many guests who have stayed at the Menger Hotel with rooms that overlook the Alamo have said that they have spotted the ghosts of the Alamo defenders. The legend states that General Andrade of the Mexican Army tried to destroy the Alamo after the Battle of San Jacinto. As he gave his troops the order to destroy the shrine, the ghosts of Travis, Bowie, and the others appeared with flaming swords, screaming, "Do not touch these walls!"
On Nacogdoches near 1604 sits a stone tower atop a hill. It is said that this tower is also haunted by ghosts from the Alamo days. Lights are often seen at the tower at night, and many believe that the tower was a lookout post for the Alamo and that the lights belong to the spirits of the sentry.

5. The Dancing Diablo — This terrible tale took place at the El Camaroncito Nite Club in the 1970s. The bar, located at 411 W. Old Highway 90, was visited by a debonair patron one evening who danced with many different women. Late in the evening, one lady looked down and noticed that the

dapper dancer had the feet of a chicken, which of course is the sign of the devil. The woman screamed, and El Diablo ran from the club.

El Camaroncito Nite Club is now closed, but the chicken-footed dancer has been reported at other establishments throughout the years.

6. The Ghosts of Milam Square — Few people realize that the public park between Santa Rosa Hospital and El Mercado was once a cemetery for the Canary Islanders. It is said that if you pass through the square with evil thoughts, you will be visited by spirits.

7. The Converse Wolfman — Many years ago in the area of Skull Creek near FM 1518, the legend of the Wolfman of Converse began. The legend tells of a thirteen-year-old boy, who spent most of his time reading, being given a rifle by his father. The father thought the boy was too much of a book worm, and he thought that by forcing the child to go hunting he could reform the youngster.

After his first day out with the gun, the boy came home and told his parents of a wolfman-type creature in the woods. The father, not believing the boy, told him to go out and not to return until he killed something. When the young hunter did not return, a search party was organized. When they reached the creek bed, the searchers found the wolfman feasting on the dead boy's body.

The wolfman supposedly returns to the creek during full moons. During his return, the water in the creek will turn blood red.

8. The Donkey Lady — Also called La Llorona, the donkey lady is condemned to a life as a ghost for drowning her children. Not only is she a ghost, but her beautiful body is topped off with the ugly head of a donkey.

The story of La Llorona is that of a beautiful poor girl who fell in love with a rich aristocrat. Because they were of different classes, they were forbidden to marry. The young lady thus became the man's mistress and bore him several children. Some versions say she drowned the children because she was poor and could not afford to keep them. Others say she drowned them because she was evil. Regardless, because of her awful actions, she was condemned to life as an unsightly ghost.

The Donkey Lady has been reported on Applewhite Road near Zarzamora and at the intersection of Blanco and Lockhill-Selma. She also has been spotted by teenagers who go to Espada Park to neck. The legend of La Llorona is often told by superstitious parents who tell their children of the ghost who haunts youngsters that play near forbidden waters.

9. The Navarro House Ghosts — This downtown landmark is the former home of Jose Antonio Navarro, signer of the Texas Declaration of Independence. Believers in the paranormal have spotted furniture that has been moved, and footsteps have been heard. Some say the ghost is the home's namesake, others say it is that of a slain prostitute, a slain bartender, or a Confederate deserter.

10. The Seven-Foot Chinese Woman — This large Asian ghost haunts an old cemetery near Stinson Field. Some tales tell of a seven-foot-tall local woman who killed herself because her Chinese contemporaries ridiculed her for being so tall. Some say she died in a fire. A bearded woman is said to haunt people in the same area.

11. Midget Mansion — This legend was fueled by the overactive imaginations of teenagers who attended Marshall and Clark high schools. An old abandoned home situated between Datapoint Drive and Medical Drive near the Medical Center was the source of this story. For years, students from the school would visit the grounds after dark to tell the story of a mansion run by evil midgets.

Nine Unusual San Antonio Outings

You have visited the Alamo, the missions, the zoo, the Institute of Texan Cultures, all the museums, and you have read the entire book, and you still cannot find anything to do. Why not try one of these unusual outings?

1. Walk the Texas Star Trail — The San Antonio Conservation Society along with the Texas Sesquicentennial Committee have created a unique walking tour of downtown. Guides to the tour can be acquired at the visitors bureau across from the Alamo. Markers inserted in the sidewalk throughout downtown make the trail easy to follow.

2. Visit the city's massive eastside cemetery complex — Take New Braunfels Avenue to Commerce Street and discover blocks of gravesites that include many of the founders of San Antonio. These gravesites date back to a time when this area was on the outskirts of the city on a hill overlooking downtown. Names such as Kampmann, Menger, Steves, and Groos can be found throughout the area. An old Confederate cemetery is hidden off Commerce Street. Texas' only Confederate general is buried there, as are 206 veterans of the Civil War, including soldiers from Germany, Scotland, France, and England who fought for the South.

Many of the city's early churches had plots in this complex. St. Joseph's Cemetery is filled with many of the German elite of early San Antonio. Clara Driscoll, savior of the Alamo, is buried in a tomb on the west edge of the cemetery just off Commerce. Sidney Brooks (Brooks Air Force Base namesake) is buried a few yards from there. A woman buried in her Ferrari is also resting somewhere amidst the graves.

San Antonio's first National Cemetery is located here. It is the final resting place of Harry Wurzbach, Lt. George Kelly, General Bullis, and a host of other familiar names. Fortunately, this is one of the few parts of the complex that is in decent shape. Many of the other plots are overgrown with weeds and have had tombstones destroyed. In the last few years, public awareness of the cemeteries has grown, and plans are being discussed to improve the facilities.

3. Dine at a converted gas station or icehouse — San Antonio may have set a record for the number of gas stations that have been converted into dining establishments. The most prominent is Little Hipp's, which is often credited for starting the trend. Located on McCullough by the Humana Hospital, Little Hipp's has been a local favorite for years.

You may also want to try Chris Madrid's on Blanco, the Sandwich Garden on McCullough, Luther's on North Main, and the Beauregard on South Alamo. All these establishments have an avid neighborhood following.

4. Discover the city's public murals — Start at the post office on Alamo Plaza. In the lobby, you will find an excellent example of Depression era art known as "Art for the Millions." The mural depicts Texas from the time of Indians to its industrialization.

Alamo Stadium features a mural of area sports. The artwork is above the main entrance. Hemisfair Plaza has a host of public murals. The outside of the arena facing the tower features the city's largest painting. Titled "Victory and Triumph," it depicts some of San Antonio's popular architectural features. The mural by Roland Rodriguez was financed by Target Stores, and their logo can be seen twice in the painting.

Inside the main concourse to the arena and above the Lila Cockrell Theatre are two pieces of artwork that were created for Hemisfair '68. They reflect the fair's theme, "A Confluence of Civilizations."

The city's west side is a great place to search for murals. Many of the area's businesses have lent the sides of their buildings to resident artists.

5. Visit an old-fashioned soda fountain — Ever have a powerful hunger for an old-fashioned ice cream soda or a chocolate malt? Why not stop at one of the many drug stores

in the city that still feature a soda fountain? The Olmos Pharmacy at the corner of Hildebrand and McCullough and Pat's Drug Store on Broadway in Alamo Heights are two of the most popular. Laurel Heights Pharmacy on Main Avenue also features an old soda fountain. The Nash on lower San Pedro is an old drug store that has been converted into a restaurant and is worth the trip. The Milam Building features an old coffee shop on its first floor that brings back some memories of an earlier time.

6. Attend a Catholic mass in one of San Antonio's many churches — Downtown San Antonio features four Catholic churches all with remarkable features. Other notable churches include the Shrine of the Little Flower and the Chapel at Our Lady of the Lake University. Many of the area churches regularly feature Mariachi masses and services in a variety of languages.

If you are looking for a more historic angle, you may want to attend mass at one of the missions. All of the historic sites are also homes to active parishes.

7. Have an ice cold beer in San Antonio's favorite bar — Located downtown at 153 E. Commerce, the Esquire Bar is a favorite local watering hole for people from all walks of life. Even though the long wooden bar is filled up with a variety of people, this local hangout could never be called a yuppie bar. Old and worn, with mariachis strolling through the narrow building, the Esquire is a throwback to the days when downtown San Antonio hosted numerous such establishments.

8. Take your kids to the park — Brackenridge Park is the city's most popular park, perhaps because of the variety of activities. The miniature train, the zoo, the skyride over Sunken Gardens, and horseback riding are some of the more popular pastimes offered.

If you are looking for something a bit different, why not take the kids to the new children's playground at Hemisfair Park. The new playground is an instant success and is usually filled with both children and parents from early morning to late after dark. (How many American cities offer a safe place for children to play in the heart of the business district?)

9. Attend a lecture — Trinity University's lecture series is open to the public and usually packs Laurie Auditorium. Speakers of nationwide prominence are often featured free to the public.

Ten Little Known Facts About San Antonio that the Author Felt Belonged in this Book

1. San Antonio is one of the few cities in the U.S.A. that has a European-style youth hostel. The hostel is often host to foreign youths who are visiting the U.S. and are accustomed to this type of accommodations. The hostel is located next to the Camp Bullis Guest House at the corner of Grayson and Pierce.

2. San Antonio has the only branch of the National Autonomous University of Mexico located outside of Mexico. The school is located at Hemisfair Park.

3. San Antonio is home to the only Maronite church in Texas. The Maronites are an Eastern Rite of the Catholic church with 700,000 members in Lebanon and 300,000 in the U.S. St. George Maronite was formed in San Antonio in 1925. The original church on the city's west side was lost to freeway construction, and in 1980 a new $1,000,000 home was built on the north side.

4. Henry Thomas, the young star of the blockbuster movie *E.T.*, is from San Antonio. Thomas was a student in the East Central school district when he made the film, and he later attended East Central High School.

5. Woodlawn Lake was originally known as West End Lake. The lake was part of a development known as West End Town, the city's first suburb. The area was connected to downtown via a trolley line. A levy was built over Alazan

Creek for the track, and the dirt came from what is now the casting pond. The lake became known as Woodlawn Lake in the 1930s.

6. Michael Nesmith of the '60s group The Monkees was a student at San Antonio College. His mother also made her mark on the world—she invented Liquid Paper.

7. Carol Burnett was born in San Antonio. She lived at 2803 West Commerce and attended Crockett Elementary School before moving west.

8. During the 1920s, San Antonio was home to the burgeoning film industry. Drawn to the Alamo City by its warm weather and variety of terrain, the moviemakers shot dozens of films here. The most successful company was the Star Film Ranch located in the old Hot Wells Hotel.

9. The city once hosted aerialists during its annual Fiesta celebration in the 1950s. The Ceptar Family of Europe performed twice daily on a highwire suspended over Houston Street. The family and other performers comprised the Zugspitzartisen troupe which would walk and ride bicycles high above Alamo Plaza without a net.

10. Burl Ives won an Oscar in 1958 for his role in *Big Country*. This has nothing to do with San Antonio, I just thought everybody should know this.

Mark Louis Rybczyk

Acknowledgements

Anybody who has ever written a historical book knows that a great amount of research is dependent on the numerous efforts of various people. I would like to thank the following without whom this book could not have been possible.

The entire San Antonio Conservation Society, without whom there would not be much to write about. Special thanks go to Mrs. Roland T. Jones and the entire staff of the Conservation Society Library.

Kathy Miller, my best friend, without whose encouragement and support my dream of writing this book could never have become a reality. Her valuable assistance in the technical areas of writing and research proved to be a godsend.

Kirk Dooley, my writing mentor, whose guidance and advice made the publication of this work possible. I am truly lucky that I met someone whose love for writing is equal to his knowledge of the publishing world. I am in your debt.

Ray Henry Zoller, who taught me to love the Tower Life Building, which eventually opened my eyes to see the beauty of downtown San Antonio. His assistance in helping me acquire an Apple IIC computer made writing a pleasure.

The entire staff of the San Antonio Library with special thanks to the historical department who made countless numbers of trips for me to the vertical files and to the rare book collection to gather materials. Despite the large volume of items I requested, they always treated me with courtesy, even at 4:45 Saturday afternoon. I would also like to thank the unknown transient who assisted me in finding information on the Alamo Bowl. After searching for over an hour with a variety of librarians, I could find nothing on this subject. Then out of the blue, a poorly dressed man found a book that listed the event. When I went to thank him he was gone. I hope his days of hard luck have ended.

Diane Bruce and Tom Shelton from the Institute of Texan Cultures. Your efforts were greatly appreciated.

The entire staff of the Fort Worth library who assisted with numerous interlibrary loans and also who have an excellent historical department.

Wallace O. Chariton and the people of Wordware Publishing who had faith in this project.

Thanks to Christine Landholt, David Arias, Frank Gonzales (the subject of many a romance novel) and "Cowboy Bob" Robert Lopez for providing lodging quite often with only moments notice. Special thanks to Mark Stewart, one of the few people who loves San Antonio as much as I do and the only person crazy enough to accompany me on some of my "fact finding" missions. To quote a mutual friend, "you must be a college boy."

To Victor Sansone, Ted Stecker, Doris Thompson, Terry Dorsey, and the entire staff of KSCS radio in Dallas for giving me the time and support to pursue this project.

Also, Donna Carroll from the St. Mary's Athletic Department, Henry Guerra, Bruce Hathaway, Dan Cook, Bo Carter of the Southwest Conference, John Bolt, George Berg, and Herman Richter.

Books on San Antonio

American Institute of Architects, San Antonio Chapter. *Historic San Antonio 1700-1900*. San Antonio: 1963.

Aniol, Claude B. *San Antonio, City of Missions*. New York: Hastings House, 1943.

Baker, T. Lindsey. *The Polish Texans*. San Antonio: The Institute of Texas Cultures, 1982.

Broussard, Ray F. *San Antonio During the Texas Republic*. El Paso: Texas Western Press, 1967.

Bushick, Frank H. *Glamorous Days in Old San Antonio*. San Antonio: Naylor Publishing, 1934.

Buck, Samuel M. *Yanaguana's Successors*. San Antonio: Naylor Publishing, 1949.

Butterfield, Jack C. *Free State of Bejar*. Austin: Daughters of Republic of Texas Library Committee, 1963.

Chabot, Frederic C. *San Antonio and Its Beginnings*. San Antonio: Naylor Publishing, 1931.

Chabot, Frederick C. *With The Makers of San Antonio*. San Antonio: Naylor Publishing, 1937.

Crook, Cornelia E. *San Pedro Springs Park*. San Antonio: Cornelia E. Crook, 1967.
Only 500 copies exist of this self-published book. Its in-depth look at the city's oldest park is surpassed by none.

Corner, William. *History of San Antonio de Bexar*. San Antonio: Bainbridge and Cooper, 1938.
One of the few books to donate so much space to the acequia system and to the layouts of the missions.

Curtis, Albert. *Fabulous San Antonio*. San Antonio: Naylor Publishing, 1955.

Everett, Donald E. *San Antonio Legacy*. San Antonio: Trinity University Press, 1979.

Driscoll, Frank A. and Grisham, Noel. *A Guide to Historic San Antonio and the Texas Border Country.* Burnet, Texas: Eakin Press, 1982.

DeZavala, Adina. *The Alamo.* San Antonio: Naylor Publishing, 1956.

Fehrenbach, T. R. *The San Antonio Story.* Tulsa: Continental Heritage Press, 1978.
Legendary Texas historian Fehrenbach has compiled an excellent timeline of the city's history. This work really captures San Antonio's spirit and its ever changing moods.

Furey, Francis F. *Archdiocese of San Antonio.* San Antonio: 1974.

Hagner, Lillie May. *Alluring San Antonio.* San Antonio: Lillie May Hagner, 1947.

Hardy, Mary Olivia. *History of Fort Sam Houston.* San Antonio: Naylor Publishing, 1951.

Henderson, Richard B. *Maury Maverick, A Political Biography.* Austin: University of Texas Press, 1970.

Heusinger, Edward W. *A Chronology of Events in San Antonio.* San Antonio: Standard Printing, 1951.

House, Boyce. *City of Flaming Adventure, The Chronicle of San Antonio.* San Antonio: Naylor Publishing, 1949.

Lomax, Louise. *San Antonio's River.* San Antonio: Naylor Publishing, 1948.
The ultimate history of the river, from the days of the missions to the early days of the River Walk.

Johnston, Leah Carter. *San Antonio, St. Anthony's Town.* San Antonio: Naylor Publishing, 1947.

Jutson, Mary Carolyn Hollers. *Alfred Giles, An English Architect in Texas and Mexico.* San Antonio: Trinity University Press, 1972.

Maguire, Jack. *Texas, Amazing But True.* Austin: Eakin Press, 1984.

Maverick, Muary. *A Maverick American.* New York: Covici, Friede Publishers, 1937.
Maverick, the former San Antonio mayor and congressman, provides a first-hand look into San Antonio in the early 20th century and into one of San Antonio's first families.

McLemore, David. *A Place In Time: A Pictorial View of San Antonio's Past.* San Antonio: Express-News Corp., 1980.
This photographic essay on San Antonio's past contains unique photos not found elsewhere.

Morrison, Andrew. *The City of San Antonio, Texas.* St. Louis: George W. Engelhardt, 1885. (Reprinted in 1977 by Norman Brock)
This book was part of the popular Engelhardt Series of Guide Books to America.

Myler, Charles Bennett. *A History of English Speaking Theatre in San Antonio Before 1900.* Diss. University of Texas, 1968.

Newcomb, Pearson. *The Alamo City.* San Antonio: Pearson Newcomb Publisher, 1926.

Odom, Marianne and Young, Gaylon Finklea. *The Businesses That Built San Antonio.* San Antonio: Living Legacies, 1985.
This effort written by the two founders of Living Legacies, a firm which specializes in recording oral histories, is one of the most fascinating books to be written on San Antonio. The book not only centers on businesses, but on the people behind them.

Ramsdell, Charles. *San Antonio, A Historical and Pictorial Guide.* Austin: University of Texas Press, 1959.
A definite must for all those interested in becoming a consummate San Antonian. The pre-1960 edition offers a unique historical perspective on the city. The recent editions offer more up-to-date information.

Ruggles, William B. *The History of the Texas League of Professional Baseball Clubs 1881-1951.* Dallas: The Texas League, 1951.

San Antonio Chapter of the American Institute of Architects. *A Guide to San Antonio Architecture.* San Antonio: SAAIA, 1987.

San Fernando Cathedral. *The Truth About The Burial Of The Remains of the Alamo Heroes.* San Antonio: Artes Graficias, 1938.
This rare book was put out by San Fernando in 1938 to quell the controversy surrounding the discovery of remains that supposedly belong to the Alamo defenders.

Schoelwer, Susan. *Alamo Images.* Dallas: Southern Methodist University Press, 1985.

Schuchard, Ernst. *100th Anniversary of the Pioneer Flour Mills*. San Antonio: The Naylor Company, 1951.

This book offers not only a history of one of the city's oldest businesses, but also numerous photos of San Antonio's early days.

Stumpf, Mrs. Franz. *San Antonio's Menger*. San Antonio: 1953.

Tengg, Nic. *Visitor's Guide and History of San Antonio, Texas*. San Antonio: Nic Tengg, 1918.

The Industries of San Antonio. San Antonio: Land & Thompson, 1885. (Reprinted in 1977 by Norman Brock)

Topperwein, Fritz A. *Footnotes of the Buckhorn*. Boerne: Highland Press Inc., 1960.

Torrente, Reverend Father Camillo. *Old And New San Fernando*. San Antonio: The Claretian Missionaries, 1927.

Turner, Leo. *The Story of Fort Sam Houston 1876-1936*. San Antonio: 1936.

Wertenbaker, Green Payton. *San Antonio*. New York: Whittlesey House, 1946.

Workers of the Writers Program of the Works Progress Administration. *The WPA Guide To Texas*. Austin: Texas Monthly Press, 1986.

Workers of the Writers Program of the Works Progress Administration. *San Antonio, An Authoritative Guide to the City and Its Environs*. San Antonio: The Clegg Company, 1938.

This Depression era booklet is part of the now hard to find American Guide Series.

Wright, Mrs. S. J. *Story of The Spanish Governor's Palace*. San Antonio: Naylor Publishing, 1932.

Wright, Mrs. S. J. *Where Lies The Heroes of The Alamo*. Dallas: Banks, Upshaw and Company, 1937.

Zunker, Vernon G. *A Dream Come True: Robert Hugman and San Antonio's River Walk*. San Antonio: 1983.

The 1987-1988 Eleventh Grade Gifted and Talented Class of Robert E. Lee High School. *The Visitor's Guide to San Antonio Architecture*. San Antonio: 1988.

Index